AF598890

CLASSIC GUNS OF THE WORLD SERIES

THE GERMAN MG 34 & MG 42 MACHINE GUNS

IN WORLD WAR II

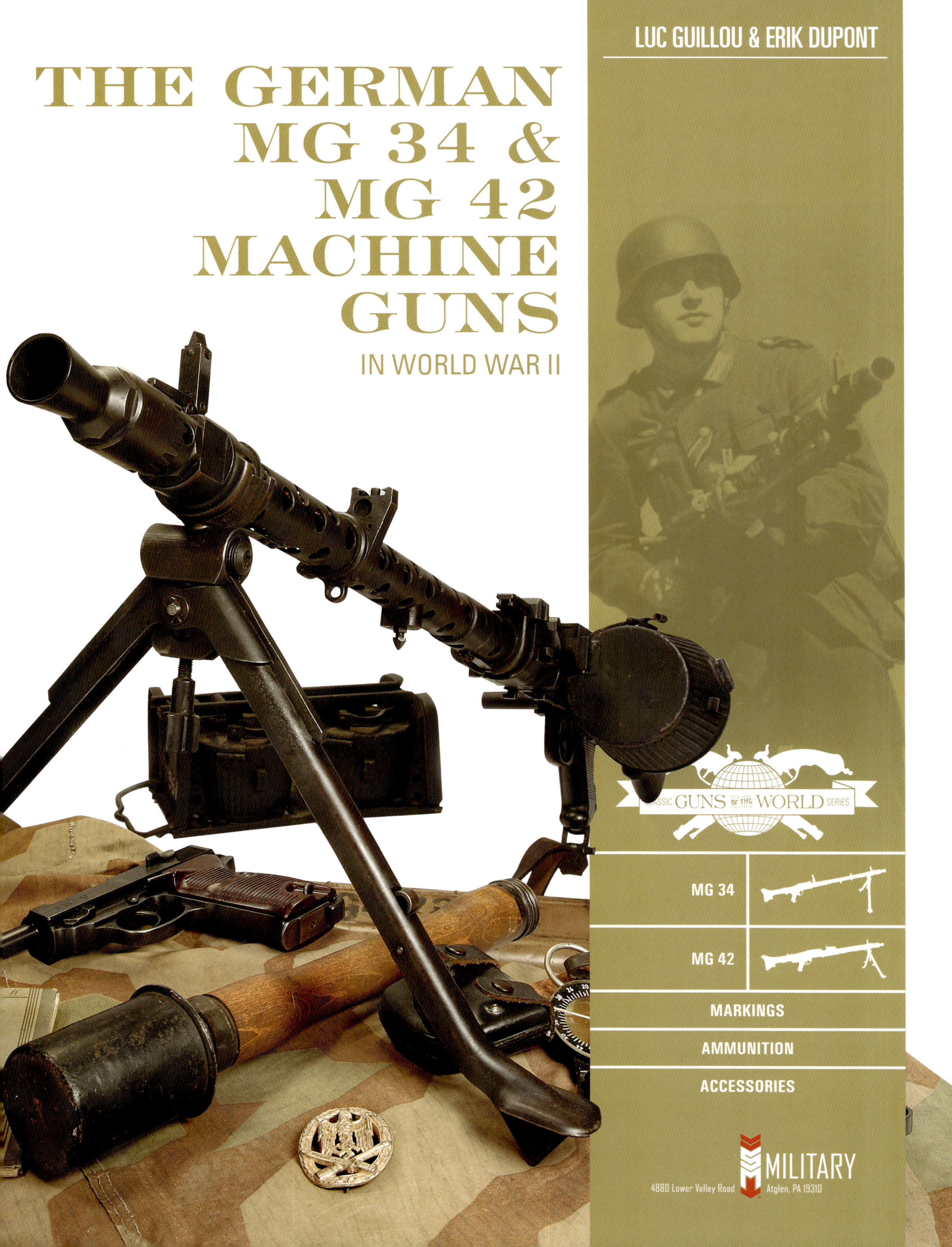

LUC GUILLOU & ERIK DUPONT
THE GERMAN MG 34 & MG 42 MACHINE GUNS
IN WORLD WAR II
CLASSIC GUNS OF THE WORLD SERIES
MG 34
MG 42
MARKINGS
AMMUNITION
ACCESSORIES
MILITARY
4880 Lower Valley Road
Atglen, PA 19310

Originally published as *Les mitrailleuses allemandes MG 34 et MG 42*
by RÉGI Arm, Paris © 2016, RÉGI Arm
Translated from the French by Julia and Frédéric Finel
Library of Congress Control Number: 2019947424

Cover design by Justin Watkinson
Type set in Helvetica Neue LT Pro/Times New Roman

ISBN: 978-0-7643-5936-1
Printed in China

Published by Schiffer Publishing, Ltd.
4880 Lower Valley Road
Atglen, PA 19310
Phone: (610) 593-1777; Fax: (610) 593-2002
E-mail: Info@schifferbooks.com
Web: www.schifferbooks.com

CONTENTS

CHAPTER 1

ORIGINS

Colorized postcard showing a Maxim MG 08 machine gun surrounded by its machine gun crew. The weapon was of a formidable efficiency, but its weight (an operational weight of around 65 kg) and its bulkiness limited its mobility during offensives. *DR*

DEVELOPMENT OF GERMAN MACHINE GUNS DURING WORLD WAR I

In 1914, the German army entered the war armed with the Maxim MG 08 water-cooled machine gun. Robust and accurate, it could endure sustained periods of firing; this machine gun was a formidable defensive weapon.

In the trench warfare that symbolized the First World War between 1915 and 1918, its presence in the fortifications of the German front line contributed to breaking many Allied offensives.

With an operational weight of 69 kg (including 4 kg of water held in the water-cooled jacket), the MG 08 was not very mobile. The German army therefore developed a lighter version of the MG 08 called the MG 08/15, which, despite its operational weight of 21 kg, was nonetheless transportable by one man.

This weapon proved to be as reliable and effective as the MG 08, but its users remained at a disadvantage in terms of mobility in relation to their French, British, or American adversaries armed with the Chauchat, Lewis, or BAR light machine guns: air-cooled weapons, weighing between 8 and 12 kg, and with a feeding system facilitating both mobility and use by one man.

The necessity of providing light machine guns with a very high firing rate for use by aviation led to the development of two remarkable machine guns: the Parabellum LMG 13 and the Bergmann LMG 15.

German aviation accorded its preference for the LMG 13 Parabellum, so the several thousand Bergmann LMG 15s that had already been produced became temporarily useless. When, in 1915, the German army launched its emergency program for the adoption of a light machine gun, these Bergmanns were retrieved and converted into infantry weapons (the program that was to end with the adoption of the MG 08/15).

The Bergmann LMG 15s, transformed into infantry machine guns, were light and easy to handle, but their light, air-cooled barrel heated up very quickly and rendered the weapon unable to be used after about 250 cartridges were fired. The standard machine guns of the German army therefore remained the MG 08 and 08/15.*

At the end of the war, an attempt was made to lighten the MG 08/15 by replacing the water-cooled jacket with a light, perforated, slotted tubular jacket. This resulted in the MG 08/18, a weapon that remained handicapped by the weight of the heavy mechanism of the MG 08/15 that it had inherited. It also had the same flaws as the Bergmann LMG 15 in regard to the heating of the barrel.

*The German army also used imported Madsen light machine guns and captured British Lewises, which meant it could appreciate the advantages of air-cooled light machine guns.

French infantrymen armed with a CSRG model 1915 "Chauchat" light machine gun. Even though rudimentary, this light (8.7 kg) and easy-to-handle weapon could be used by one man, giving the French attack waves considerable fire power. *DR*

The "light" MG 08/15 machine gun was the answer to the Chauchat and the Lewis in service in the Allied armies. With a mass of around 18 kg when in operation, this water-cooled weapon remained, however, much less mobile than the Allied light machine guns. *DR*

In the midwar period, the German army also envisaged the adoption of a multipurpose weapon derived from the MG 08/15: the LMG 16. This was simply an MG 08/15 with no bipod, where the butt was replaced by a firing handle. This weapon was mounted on a model 16 tripod (lighter tripod mount, designed to replace the heavy sledge mount of the MG 08).

The weapon was not really adjustable, since its transformation back into an MG 08/15 required the intervention of a unit armorer. However, its adoption showed the advantage of being able to make all types of automatic service weapon based on one mechanism and, above all, would have simplified the training of machine gunners by limiting their instruction to a single type of mechanism.

The difficulty of transforming the MG 08 and 08/15 production lines for the production of the LMG 16 during the course of the war meant this promising project could not be followed up on. However, the LMG 16 opened up a line of thought that would later give rise to the concept of the "universal machine gun" (*Einheitsmaschinengewehr*), which was to be formalized in the 1920s by an officer of the Herreswaffenamt, Major von Weber.

MACHINE GUNS OF THE REICHSWEHR

The German defeat of 1918 and the subsequent revolution put an end to research on the subject of machine guns for a period of time. The Treaty of Versailles forbade research in this area in German territory; German factories acquired subsidiaries abroad so as to develop their projects in peace. This period gave German manufacturers the necessary thinking time to perfect the idea of a universal machine gun—simply making the components lighter was not sufficient to resolve the problem.

To remedy the problem of the inevitable heating of a light, air-cooled barrel, it was also necessary to design a weapon on which the barrel could be changed rapidly, and another priority was the development of a new type of light, easily transportable mount. The mount nonetheless had to be able to absorb the vibrations of automatic fire, to ensure accurate firing.

At the end of the First World War, the German army tried an air-cooled version of the MG 08/15: the MG 08/18. This weapon, with a narrow barrel that heated up rapidly, proved incapable of carrying out sustained fire. The barrel-slotted tubular jacket on the MG 08/18 already heralded those of future German MG 13 and MG 34 machine guns. We see here an MG 08/18 fitted with a blank firing device, in service in the Finnish forces between the two world wars. *DR*

The Bergmann light machine gun LMG 15 had been initially developed as an aviation machine gun. It was, however, replaced in this regard by the Parabellum MG 13. Those LMG 15s unused by the aviation branch were converted into light infantry machine guns. Even though the lightness and handling ability of these weapons gave them great flexibility in this role, their light barrel heated up too quickly and therefore could be used only for short-duration fire. *DR*

On this last point, German technicians closely studied the foldable tripod developed by the Danish company Madsen for its light machine gun. When this soft-mount was folded, it could be transported by one man like a knapsack.

In addition, it was fitted with a spring shock absorber that absorbed the recoil of the weapon; this gave it good stability despite its lightness. It was also fitted with a remote firing control, meaning the user could activate the trigger while being less exposed to enemy fire.

The weapons designers also had to take into account technical innovations that had arisen for the Great War. The future machine gun of the Reichswehr had to be mounted on armored or nonarmored vehicles and be used for defensive strikes against aircraft, which necessitated an adjustable rate of fire from 800 to 1,000 shots per minute, whereas a rate in the order of 600 shots per minute was required for antipersonnel fire.

While waiting to have a machine gun that responded perfectly to specifications, the Reichswehr was compelled to replace a part of worn or damaged MG 08-15s by a more modern machine gun. To this end it adopted a weapon proposed by the Rheinmetal company, which had bought the old Dreyse firm workshops in Sömmerda in 1901.

For reasons that are not clear, this weapon was christened MG 13. This name is explained perhaps by its relation to the Dreyse model 1912 machine gun: a weapon that aspired to dethrone the MG 08 and that had some of its principles of operation preserved on the MG 13, but that was not adopted by the German army. Another theory concerning its name favors the wish to deceive the Military Inter-Allied Commission of Control concerning its development, by convincing them that the figure "13" indicated a commissioning date prior to 1914.

Even though the weapon had been designed by Rheinmetal, the manufacture of the MG 13 was ensured by Simson & Co., the only German enterprise authorized by the Allies to make weapons of war for the Reichswehr. It was an air-cooled weapon and was fed by a magazine that kept the short barrel recoil principle of Maxim machine guns, which the German army seemingly considered to be more reliable than gas-operated models.

On the MG 13, the change of barrel required the extraction of the bolt mechanism by the rear of the receiver. The operation therefore was hardly any quicker than on an MG 08/15 and posed the problem of the mechanism clogging up after being extracted and placed on the ground in a battlefield.

On the other hand, the MG 13 was equipped with a trigger permitting the use of a firing-mode selector, as well as a folding butt, bipod, and foresight, which facilitated its transport.

Weighing "only" 12 kg and fed by a twenty-five-round magazine, it could easily be used by one man. An ingenious system of semicircular guideways surrounding the tubular jacket, with cooling slots on the barrel, meant the bipod could be mounted either in a forward or rear position.

The military development of aviation during the First World War meant that machine guns had to be adapted for a totally unplanned function at the beginning of the war: firing at aircraft. Here is an MG 08 mounted for this purpose, on a field-made mounting. *DR*

MG 13 machine gun, equipped with its rare "type Z" drum magazine, next to its gunner's tool pouch, a canvas magazine pouch, a tool for loading magazines, and a camouflaged case for transporting magazines. The P. 08 was the standard for the machine gunner to ensure his personal protection. In the midwar period, some P.38s were also supplied.
Photo by Marc de Fromont, Musée Royal de l'armée Bruxelles Collection

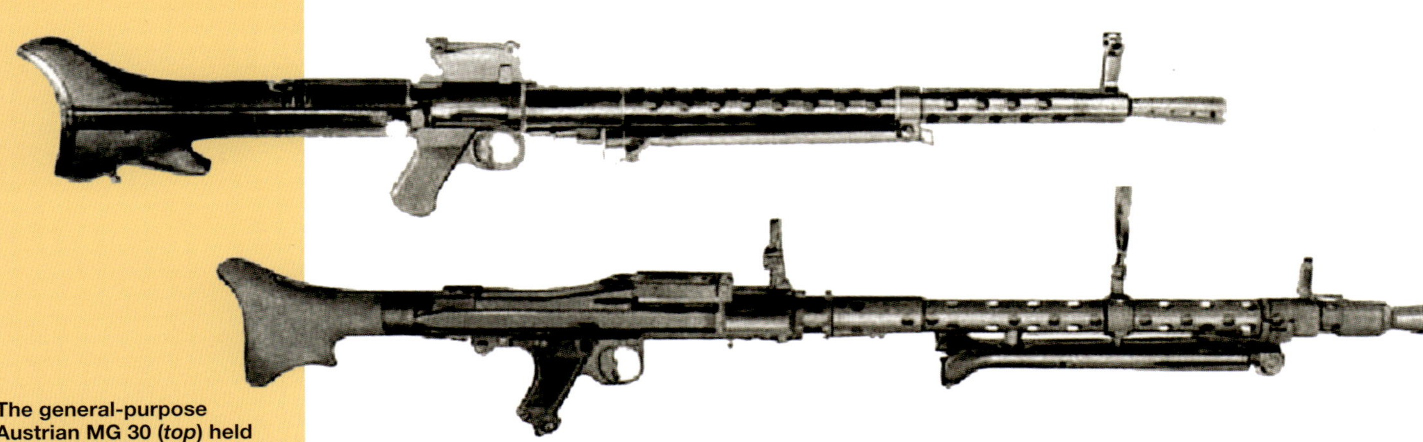

The general-purpose Austrian MG 30 (*top*) held the interest of the Reichswehr, and its design inspired that of the future German MG 34 machine gun (*bottom*). *DR*

In order to respond to the will of German high command to equip its forces with a general-purpose light machine gun, adapted to antiaircraft fire and being mounted on vehicles, the Dreyse company secretly developed the MG 13 machine gun, which was adopted as a "universal machine gun" (*Einheits-maschinengewehr*) by the Reichswehr. The weapon here is equipped with a rare "type Z" large-capacity magazine, since it had become apparent that firing only very many cartridges constituted effective antiaircraft fire. This subsequently led to magazines giving way to feeding by ammunition belts. *DR*

It also was rapid to set up and dismantle on the mounts of motorized vehicles, which were becoming more common in modern armies. This system also permitted the weapon to be set up on the turrets of armored tanks, on light vehicles, or on fortifications.

By using an adapter piece that was mounted in the fixation rails at the rear of the bipod, the MG 13 could be set up on the MG 08/15 antiaircraft tripod, to carry out firing against planes. For this purpose, Simson also marketed a tripod that was lighter but quite unstable and that was made for export to Portugal, where the MG 13 was adopted in 1938.

Neither of these tripod mounts had the required stability or handling ability for the MG 13 to be used as a fixed-position "heavy" machine gun. The Reichswehr carried out test firing with the weapon mounted on the foldable Madsen-type mounts, but did not adopt any model since none corresponded exactly to what was required.

The A7V heavy German tank was armed with a 57 mm field gun and five Maxim MG 08 machine guns. When assault tanks entered service during the First World War, it forced the technical departments of the different armed services to design machine guns able to be mounted on the armored-vehicle firing posts. *DR*

In total contradiction with its wishes to be equipped with a single machine gun, the Reichswehr, whose numbers were limited to 100,000 men, found itself equipped with four models of machine gun simultaneously:

- three "light" machine guns: the MG 08/15, MG 08/18, and MG 13

- a "heavy" machine gun: the MG 08 (some of which were mounted on the model 1908 sledge mount and others on the model 1916 tripod)

MG 13 machine gun mounted on a sidecar of the Reichswehr. Note that this weapon is equipped with a wooden fixed butt, highly unusual on this model. Thanks to the all-terrain capacities of these motorcycles with sidecars, this type of mounting meant it could be transported rapidly to any point in the battlefield where immediate fire support was necessary. *Marc de Fromont*

Austrian mountain troops using an MG 30. *DR*

It is important to clarify a point on the vocabulary used here.

Some readers will perhaps be surprised to see the MG 08 machine gun christened as a "heavy machine gun," when this weapon fired an infantry rifle cartridge. It is simply a question of using the German army terminology of the period: *Schweres Maschinengewehr*, the name chosen for weapons mounted on a heavy mount principally used for defending positions. It was during the period between the wars that the term "heavy machine gun" started to take on another meaning, designating large-caliber weapons (12.7 mm, 13.2 mm, etc.), which started to appear at that time. Initially the adjective "heavy" qualified the weight of the weapon, whereas later it was used to indicate its caliber.

It is surprising to us today that the German army adopted the MG 13, since it did not fulfill the army's wish to equip itself with one single model of general-purpose machine gun. The adoption of this weapon in reality constituted a stage of development just as much as a temporary solution, permitting the replacement of worn MG 08/15s by new weapons while conserving the specialist know-how of the Simson company technicians and in supporting this unique supplier of weapons to the Reichswehr.

Although Simson & Co. was the only German war arms manufacturers authorized to continue operations by the Allies, many inventors and manufacturers continued working in secret on projects of this type while benefiting from the discreet financing and support of the Reichswehr.

In addition, opposition to the Military Inter-Allied Commission of Control to research into machine guns was constantly circumvented by major German weapons companies by systematically engaging in "delocalization" before the term existed.

In this way, Rheinmetal had its prototypes made in Austria by the Steyr Daimler Puch A. G. company and in Switzerland by a company that it had bought in Solothurn. Mauser operated in the same way by using the services of a shell company set up in Kreutzlingen, Switzerland.

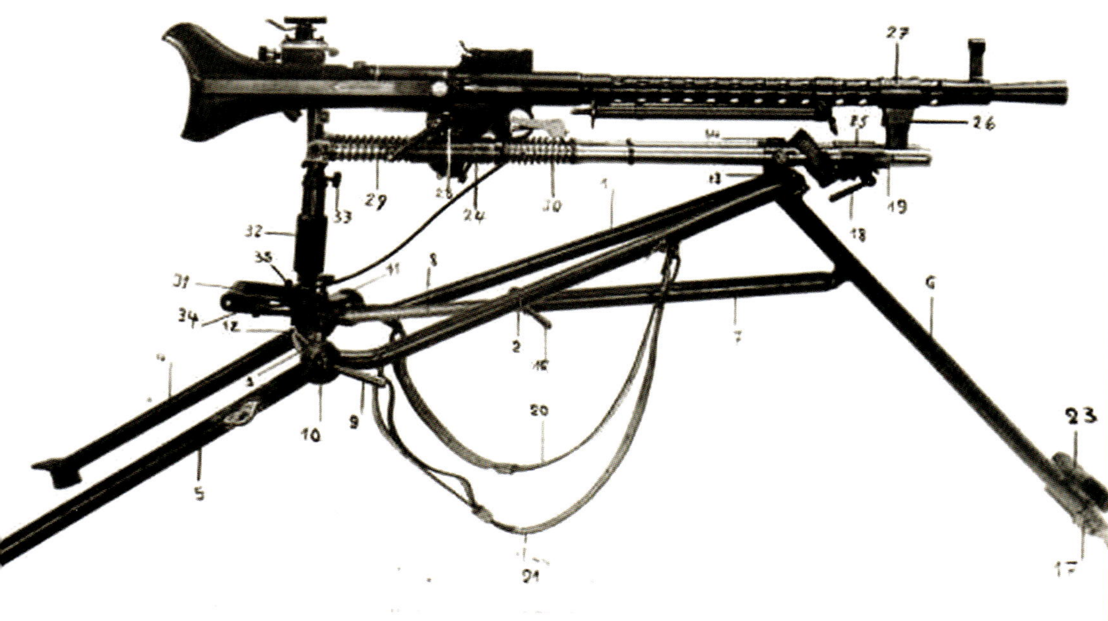

Adjustable mount for the MG 30 Solothurn, used to transform the MG 30 light machine gun into a fixed-position heavy machine gun. The principle of this mount was kept by the Reichswehr for the replacement of the MG 13: the MG 34. *DR*

Magnificent early MG 34 BSW made in 1937. This first type of example is characterized by a gas evacuation of the flash hider, pierced with three oblong holes, by a type MG 13 bipod, by its "four hole" barrel tubular jacket (between the bipod bracket and the antiaircraft sight bracket), by its worn top cover as well as by its handle for adjusting firing speed, and by its wooden butt.

This early MG 34 on its "Lafette" 1938–type mount (this example is not yet fitted with the sheet metal baffle to deflect ejected cases, nor does it have the spare bolt box). The weapon has been placed in position here behind a large tree stump. Users have fitted an MG 34 sight and periscope. The ammunition belt is positioned in the feed tray of the MG only when necessary.

Because of these ruses, the head weapons designer at Rheinmetal, Louis Stange, was able to develop a machine gun christened "MG S2-200." This weapon was fitted with an original nonrotating bolt locking; in the rear it has locking lugs on each side. The barrel has a rotary collar with internal-thread-locking grooves, moving back and forward during firing.

The chamber of the weapon had a locking collar receiving the bolt thread lugs.

This system would go on to inspire the designers of the future MG 34 machine gun, which would mount the rollers on the head of the bolt and ensure locking by the rotation of the bolt and not by that of the barrel.

This rotation locking was particularly interesting since it resolved the question of the rapid change of barrel, which was impossible with weapons having a barrel screwed in the support of the bolt, as on the MG 08/15 or the MG 13.

The MG S2-200 was adopted in 1930 by Austria in 8 × 50 R Mannlicher caliber under the name MG 30, and in 1931 by Hungary in caliber 8 × 56 R under the name MG 31.

Fed by box magazines, the MG 30 and 31 were badly adapted to firing against aircraft, leading Louis Stange to develop the MG S3-200 in 1932: a version of the MG S2-200 fed by cartridge belts. This system allowed for a greater firing capacity than with magazines. During this period, with pressure from the Military Inter-Allied Commission of Control having virtually disappeared, the general staff of the Reichswehr could at last carry out a series of different tests on machine guns on German soil.* The machine guns in competition were Simson, Gustloff, Rheinmetal, and Mauser.

The Mauser MLG 32 and the MG S3-200 of Rheinmetal ended up as favorites. The final choice of the German army, now known as the Wehrmacht, was the S3-200, which was adopted under the name MG 34 on November 1, 1935. Both companies had also developed effective light tripods ("Lafette" in German), permitting the transformation of their light machine guns into "heavy" ones.

These mounts offered sufficient stability during automatic firing to be able to use an optical sight. The model adopted by the Wehrmacht in 1934 (Lafette 34) was designed so that when activated, the searching fire device would automatically index up and down as the gun recoiled within its cradle. This ingenious system of automatic mowing down, able to be disengaged at will, made the Lafette 34 the most elaborate mount ever adopted.

The MG 34 resulted in a prototype developed by Rheinmetal but had elements inspired by the inventions of technicians from other firms, such as Mauser, Simson, and Gustloff, as well as the principles studied by independent inventors such as Heinrich Vollmer.

The official putting into service of this weapon was decided definitively only in 1939, after a period of testing in combat units carried out in 1936 and a probationary period from the end of 1938 to January 1939.

In the first instance, the new machine gun was covered by the strictest military secret, along with the first instruction notices, which were highly classified. It was of course forbidden for German soldiers to show the new weapon to foreign defense attachés, to photograph them, or even to make sketches of them.

The outbreak of the Second World War in September 1939 rapidly changed this state of affairs by making the MG 34 one of the most photographed weapons by war correspondents of the Wehrmacht.

A beautiful propaganda photograph with an MG gunner firing from the hip. In reality, the bipod unattached from the barrel jacket should normally be held in the left hand so as to have more control during firing. *DR*

* The MG 13 tests had had to take place in the USSR.

CHAPTER 2

PRESENTATION OF THE MG 34

The MG 34 can be broken down into seven elements:

- barrel
- barrel jacket and bipod
- receiver
- butt
- moving bolt and recoil spring
- feeding system
- trigger mechanism

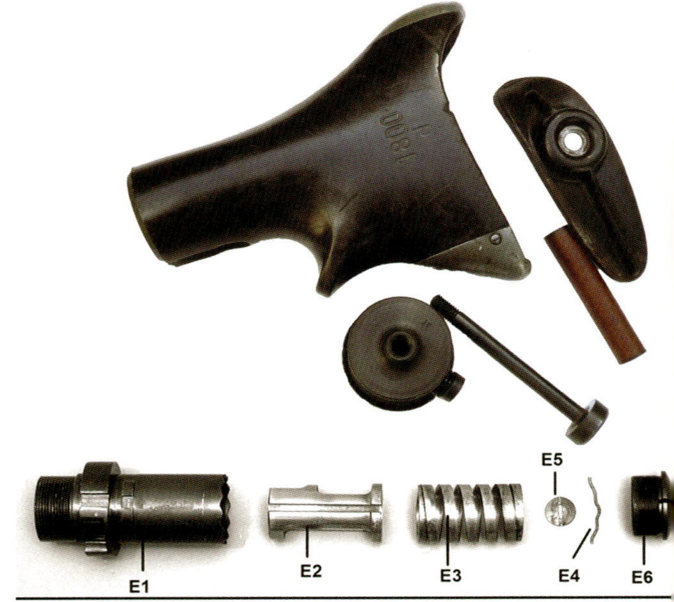

Totally disassembled early-made butt in Bakelite. Note the steel reinforcement cups mounted on the toe and heel of the butt stock, to prevent breakage.

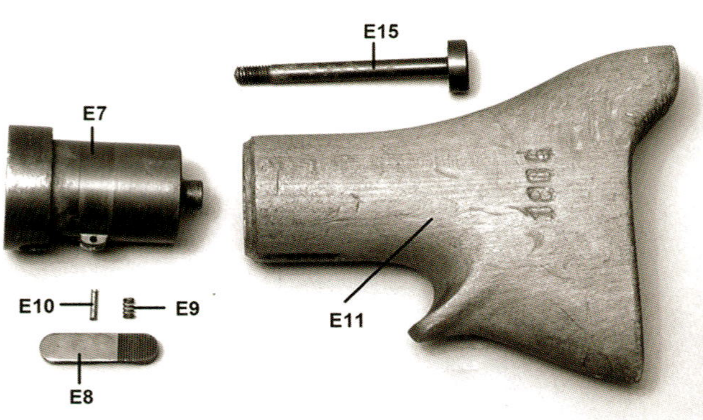

Buffer and other parts of the butt.

The barrel. With a length of 627 mm, the barrel has five grooves from the muzzle, designed to receive any residue as a result of firing. This residue is housed there under the action of the thrust of gas exerted by the recoil booster cylinder. At the rear it is screwed and pinned in a part named "barrel-locking piece," in which the head of the moving bolt is housed.

This rear part is made up of the following:

A *Gerbirgsjäger* (mountain soldier) carrying out maintenance on his MG 34 at the barracks. The jacket and its bipod have been painted white so as to be camouflaged in the snow.

- on its external surface, two guide lugs positioned on either side, which ensure the assembly of the barrel in the water-cooled jacket
- on its internal part are two cams of the two mobile head runners; the bolt head locks here by a semirotational movement

The water-cooled jacket and bipod. The water-cooled jacket is perforated with circular orifices that facilitate the cooling of the barrel. The number and arrangement of these orifices varied depending on the period of production.

At its forward part, the barrel jacket has threads in order to fix the recoil booster housing. This part is itself threaded to receive a flash hider.

At its rear part, a screwed barrel jacket bears

Early MG 34 machine gun, recognizable by its barrel jacket perforated with four holes forward of the support bracket for the antiaircraft firing sight. Surrounding the weapon are some accessories used for indirect fire: an MG.Z 34 optic with its transport case, a battery box to light the sight, a *Messdreieck* (measuring triangle) for reading firing parameters, and a map holder. *Photo by Marc de Fromont, Musée Royal de l'armée Bruxelles Collection*

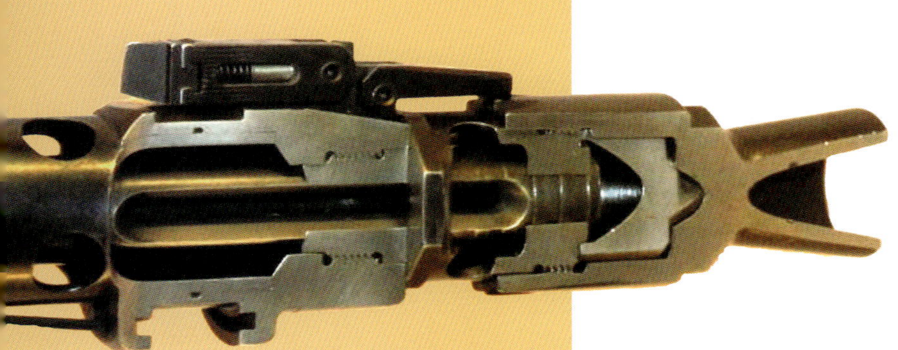

Photo of recoil booster cylinder and booster cone on an MG 34, used for training purposes, belonging to the collection of the Army Museum of Prague. This photo shows the complexity of machining required to make a MG 34. *Museum of Prague Collection*

the flash-hider latch and the folding foresight, the antiaircraft ring sight support along with the semicircular rear housing of the bipod, and the bipod-mounting groove.

Farther to the rear:

- The guide lug, allowing the folded bipod to hook under the water-cooled jacket for transport purposes, a second semicircular bipod housing, and its locking piece. This housing can be used and mounted in different configurations. The technical specifications stipulated that this machine gun had to be extremely versatile
- The second bracket is used for mounting on a vehicle, on an antiaircraft tripod, with the antiaircraft extension of the "Lafette 34" mount, or simply for moving the bipod to a central position, thereby allowing the user to cover more angles

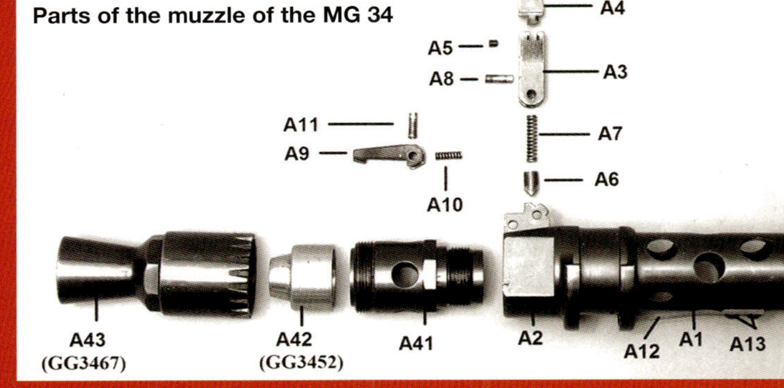

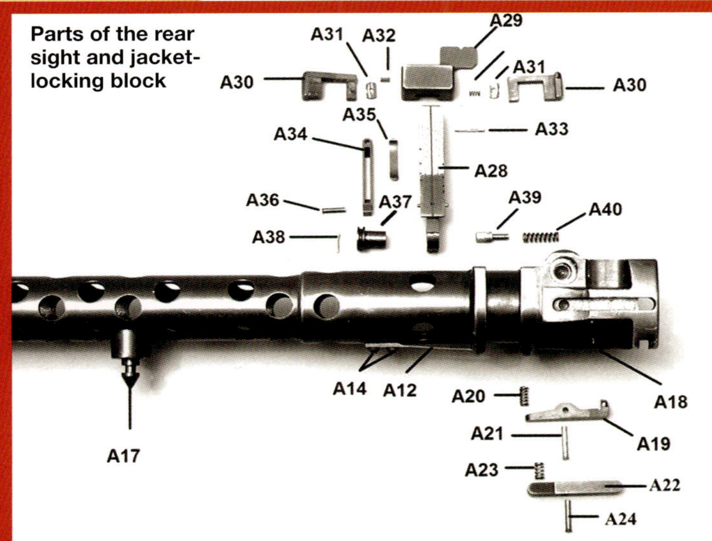

A section at the rear of the water-cooled jacket comprises the following:

- *at the left*, the bolt catch with its pin, catch, and spring
- *above and to the left*, the sight, regulated from 200 to 2,000 meters by hectometers
- *at the rear of the sight*, a foldable rear sight for antiaircraft fire
- *on the right*, a stud is inserted into the support channel on the right-hand side, and the locking catch for the connecting stud is depressed as the barrel assembly is swung onto the receiver
- *on the inside*, the housing of the barrel-locking piece, the two openings, and the two bolt-locking shoulders

At the rear part, the assembly slide of the receiver.

The bipod is made up of

- two articulated braces under a half bracket,
- a screw for adjusting the spread of the braces (this screw is absent on certain end-of-production bipods), and
- a system for locking the braces for transport.

The receiver group. Elements to note on this part from front to rear:

- The connection stud on the barrel jacket has a circular clearance to allow for the movement of the retainer, as well as a continuous threading for locking on the barrel jacket

Carrying the MG 34 the regulation way on the shoulder, holding the grip. The MG 34 is supplied with fifty cartridges contained in a drum.

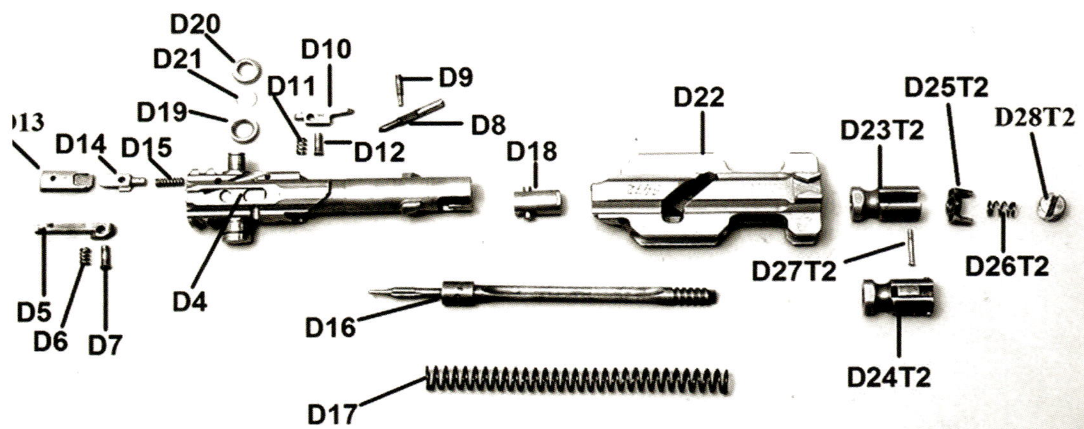

A completely disassembled bolt with a first type of firing-pin bolt

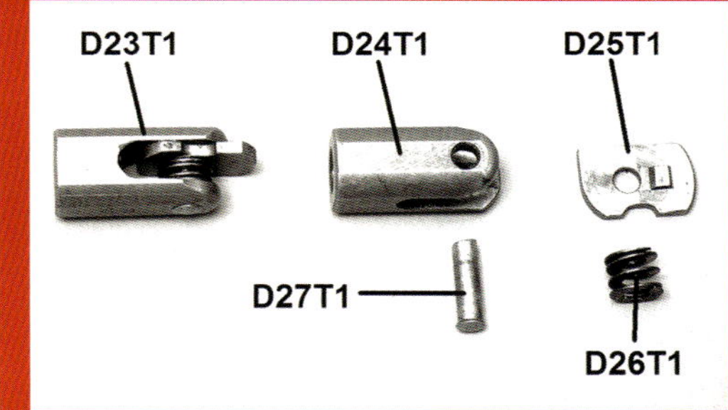

Second type of firing-pin bolt

- The top cover pin forms a lever for the disassembly of the connection stud on the magazine feed tray
- On the upper part of the receiver is a housing for the feed tray
- On the right: the ejection plate fixed by two pointed screws
- Above, the ejection port with its flap, safety, sear lever, spring and pin
- At the rear cross axe with two lugs to fix the part on the tripod mount, the buffer catch, and on the cocking handle
- On the inside; the rollers guiding the bolt, a continuous thread to fix the buffer, two helical locking and unlocking slides on the bolt, the barrel compensating spring and its catch
- On the right side the notch for the movement of the cocking handle

The butt. This has two parts:

- The butt itself, in wood or Bakelite that could be reinforced with metallic pieces at its toe and heel. It has the buffer of the rear part and its lock and spring.

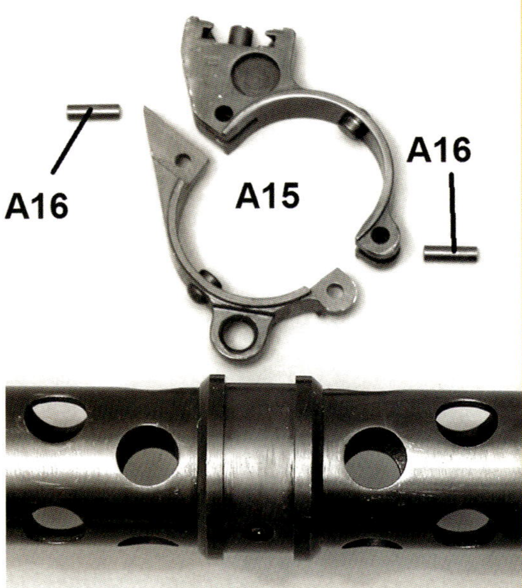

Ring for the antiaircraft sight

SS section during combat. The man on the left carries the Dreibein 34 on a belt and holds a P. 08 for personal defense.

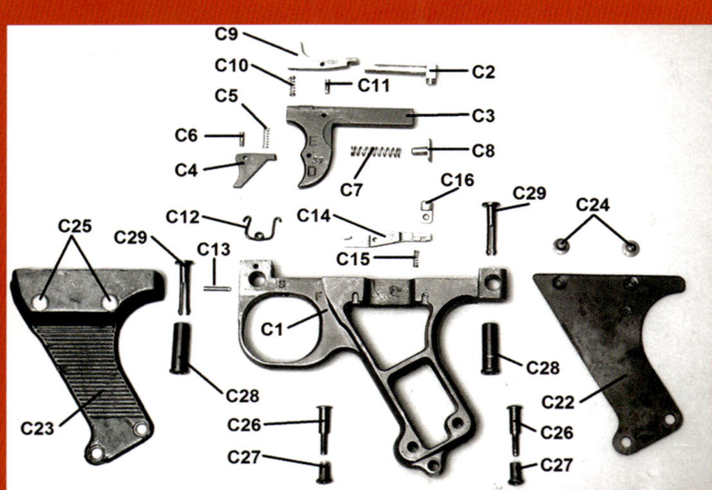

Second type of trigger mechanism and grip

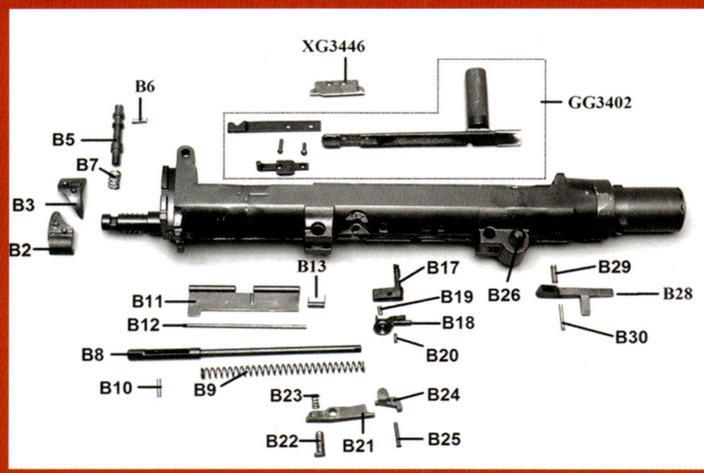

Parts of the receiver group

MG 34 rear sight

- The rear part includes the shock absorber, which is divided into two parts: the recoil spring and its sliding buffer. In the rear part the recoil spring is supported and, in this part, a continuous thread is machined, used for the assembly of the butt in the receiver. Here there are also two retainer lugs on the rear part of the butt, recoil spring housing cap, and its pin

The moving bolt and its recoil spring. The moving bolt is divided into two parts: the body of the bolt and the mobile head.

The bolt assembly consists of two main parts, the bolt head and the bolt carrier. The bolt head holds the extractor and the ejector, the cartridge stripper, the firing pin assembly, and the firing-pin release. It also has two integral short shafts, one on each side, each of which holds a pair of locking and unlocking rollers.

The body of the bolt has the following:

- on the interior, the housing of the mobile head tail, with its two indentations forming a rail for locking
- underneath, the cocking catch
- above, the housing in the shape of an "X" for the passage of the flanges for the feed lever
- at the rear part, the housing of the case, used as a disassembly tool

Mobile head. From the front to the rear: the striker hole, extractor housing, its latch and spring, the ejector and its stop pin, the locking flanges, guiding rollers, the firing-pin latch with its pin and spring, the spiral locking guides, the mobile head thrust stop (to its "armed" position), rear locking and unlocking studs, and indentations for the firing-pin stop.

On the interior: the firing-pin hole, the firing pin and its spring, the firing-pin stop, the barrel jacket, and its stop lever.

The recoil spring: 440 mm long and with forty-three loops.

The feeding mechanism. It is composed of the cover and its feeding components, with the magazine housing the following:

- The top cover for the belt feed, which holds both the feed block assembly and the feed arm and feed arm extension in place.
- The top cover latch is spring loaded and located at the rear of the top cover.

The feed block assembly, consisting of several different parts, feeds the ammo belt into the weapon, in connection with the belt feed lever and extension. The feed block itself holds the cartridge pressure pawls and the belt holding pawls, two of each in mixed pairs.

The trigger mechanism. This is composed of the trigger support, with its trigger guard and pistol grip at the front and rear; the two holes for the passing of the tubular fixation pins on the receiver, at the front; and the ejection port cover spring, at the rear.

On the interior: the trigger for single-shot fire and continuous-burst fire, and the body of the trigger, with the sear, the sear lever, the trigger plunger and its spring, the divider and its spring, and the effacement plunger.

The manufacture of the MG 34 required careful machining using first-rate materials, and its use necessitated meticulous maintenance since the weapon did not cope well with sandy or dusty conditions. Its complexity also meant that its users had to receive very thorough training.

The imperatives of productivity and economy during wartime coupled with the necessity of training more and more men motivated the German High Command to look into replacing the MG 34 with a weapon that was easier to make and use.

Features	
Caliber	7.92 mm
Ammunition	Infantry cartridge (7.92 × 57 mm)
Weapon weight	12 kg
Weight of the mount	19 kg
Theoretical rate of fire	approx. 900 shots per minute
The necessity of changing the overheated barrel after firing 250 continuous shots in reality reduced this purely theoretical rate of fire.	
Sight graduated up to 2,000 m	
Effective firing range on tripod and telescopic sight	3,500 m
Effective firing range with bipod	1,200 m

This research came to a conclusion in 1942 with the adoption of the MG 42. The putting into service of the MG 42 did not relegate the MG 34 to second place; quite the opposite. The MG 42 was appreciated for its simplicity and reliability, but the MG 34 had the advantage of being more efficient concerning ammunition. In addition, the 34 model had a system for changing the barrel that was compatible for use with armored vehicles or fortress mounts; such was not the case for the 42.

This photo reproduces the field repair of a weapon temporarily put out of action by a firing incident. Once the belt is removed and the weapon is on safety, the receiver group is swung around to extract the barrel. The elements of the leather tool kit of the weapon can be seen.

CHAPTER 3

USE AND OPERATION OF THE MG 34

Close-up of the complex machining and the high quality of the linking piece of the cooling jacket to the receiver group

Firing generally took place in a lying-down position with the machine gun on its bipod. This is the most common position since it offers a fast setup time while giving maximum cover. The shooter was nonetheless trained to use his weapon at the hip or placed on the shoulder of a comrade, depending on the circumstances.

USE

To set up the weapon, the firer presses the two lateral latches positioned at the bottom of the bipod so as to unlock the retaining stud from the barrel jacket, then positions the weapon on the ground, facing the objective. He adjusts the height of the bipod by means of changing the angle of the legs in relation to the configuration of the terrain and his firing position.

After taking care to put the foresight and backsight in a vertical position, and adjusting the backsight to the distance of the target, the weapon can be put to the shoulder. The weapon is held by grasping the grip with the right hand and placing the left hand crosswise under the buttstock.

While the shooter is getting into position, the ammunition handler opens an ammunition box and puts a cartridge belt in the weapon. The cartridge belts usually have a starter end (commonly called a "belt tab"), meaning that the weapon can be fed without having to open the top cover (which improves the setup time).

It is sufficient to introduce the starter end in the feeding port on the left side of the weapon by pushing it until it appears on the other side. The gunner then grasps the end of the belt tab on the right side of the weapon and tugs it toward the right until the belt is blocked by a click-and-lock system and the first cartridge reaches the retainer on the magazine housing.

To feed the MG with belts with no belt tabs, it is sufficient to remove the first two cartridges, open the cover, and position the belt in the magazine housing, with the first cartridge on the holding pawls on the retainer, then to close the cover while pulling toward the right on the two links lacking a cartridge, so as to maintain the belt in the correct position.

With the weapon being fed, the shooter brings the cocking handle toward the rear; as a result of the rear movement of the bolt, the ejection port cover placed under the receiver opens automatically. When the cocking handle finishes its movement, the receiver catches the trigger head. The last maneuver consists of bringing back the cocking handle to its initial position until it clicks and locks on the receiver. The handle will remain immobile during firing of the belt.

The weapon is now loaded and armed; firing can commence.

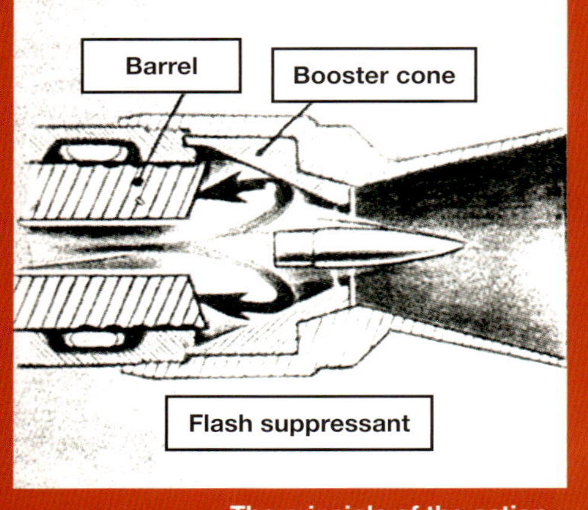

The principle of the action of gas on the front of the barrel on the interior of the "recoil booster cylinder"

Front view of the cooling jacket; this version has three holes, with a gas recoil booster cone with cylindrical holes. The bipod is supplied with a brace at the top of each leg.

After identifying the target, the gunner checks that the safety is in "fire" position, then presses the upper section of the trigger for single-shot fire (E = *Einzelfeuer*), and the lower section of the trigger for full automatic fire (D = *Dauerfeuer*).

After virtually continuous firing of around 250 cartridges, the barrel reaches such a temperature that it must be replaced (the instructions were to change the barrel after emptying a box of ammunition). It should be noted that to control the weapon on its bipod and to maximize firing accuracy, the users were trained to press the trigger briefly in order to fire just three or four rounds each time.

To change the barrel, the gunner moves back the grip until the bolt catches the trigger, then puts the safety in the "S" position. While the assistant gunner prepares a new box of ammo belts, the firer unlocks the barrel jacket from the barrel and then swings the receiver 180 degrees to the right. This movement allows the barrel to be freed from the jacket, and it can be extracted within a few seconds.

Because the barrel is very hot, it is held by a belt tab during extraction. To take the barrel, the hand must be protected by a rag or, even better, by a wad of asbestos-covered material, supplied with the accessory kit worn on the belt. This swinging movement of the receiver is the same one used to replace the barrel when the weapon is used on a bipod. If the weapon is mounted on its Lafette mount, it is the barrel jacket that is swung to the right by the assistant gunner positioned on this side of the weapon, using the mechanism on the mount.

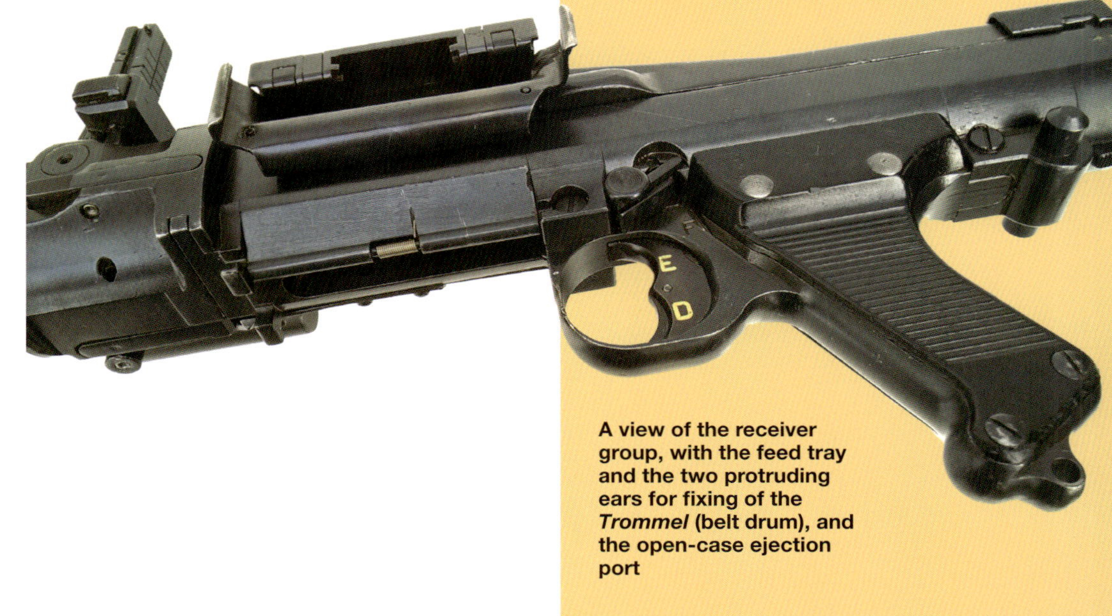

A view of the receiver group, with the feed tray and the two protruding ears for fixing of the *Trommel* (belt drum), and the open-case ejection port

Bottom view with the ejection port cover closed. This cover opens automatically when the breech is moved back via the cocking handle.

The Crimea, 1941. Using an MG 34 on a Lafette in the process of being folded up. The weapon has fired several hundred rounds judging by the number of cases and empty belts on the ground.

Method of changing the barrel on an MG 34.

1. The firer brings the bolt to an armed position.
2. The assistant gunner swings the jacket/barrel unit to the right with the Lafette lever.
3. The firer uses the belt tab to begin extracting the overheated barrel.
4. The assistant gunner, with an asbestos-treated cover protecting his left hand, then removes the barrel completely from the jacket and puts it in the *Laufschützer* (spare barrel container), where the burning-hot barrel can start to cool down.

Simultaneously with the right hand, the assistant gunner brings the cold barrel, which the firer then inserts in the jacket and locks in place.

The firer then replaces the hot barrel with a spare one, which another member of the crew has placed on his right in the spare barrel container, left in an open position.

The hot barrel is placed in the open barrel container to allow it to cool down.

Once the barrel is changed and the jacket is put back and locked, the assistant gunner feeds the weapon with the new belt. The firer activates the cocking handle, and firing can recommence.

OPERATION

The operation has two phases:

First phase: recoil of the mobile assembly (barrel-moving bolt)

The agents of the recoil movement are

1. the force of the cartridge that has just been fired, and
2. the gas accumulating in the booster cone, which exerts pressure on the forward section of the barrel.

View of a midproduction MG 34. The cooling jacket has lost a series of holes in its midsection, the cover is in pressed steel, and the buttstock, in Bakelite, no longer has metallic braces.

During recoil, the following operations take place:

Unlocking: the pressure exerted by the striker hole on the base of the fired cartridge combined with that of the gas accumulated in the recoil accelerator chamber (forward of the flash hider) on the front section of the barrel, cause the latter to move back solid with the bolt assembly over a length of 8 mm. Both bolt head rollers then come into contact with the helical receiver unlocking rails and force the bolt to turn to the left, unlocking the barrel.

Withdrawal of the firing pin: During unlocking, both rear mobile head locking studs act on the rails of both helical notches on the bolt carrier. The firing pin, solid with the hammer via the intermediary of the jacket, is carried towards the rear causing its withdrawal.

Arming of the firing pin: At the end of the withdrawal, the firing pin collar positions itself behind the firing pin latch, holding the hammer spring compressed.

Opening of the bolt: After the four locking lugs on the moving head are clear of their respective housings, they position themselves in the smooth sectors facing the guideways of the receiver. As the gas continues to push the base of the fired cartridge against the striker hole on the bolt head, this separates from the barrel and continues its recoil movement, whereas the barrel returns under the effect of its own compensating spring.

Extraction: The cartridge that has been fired is led by the extractor in the recoil movement of the bolt, which strips it from the chamber.

Ejection: During the recoil of the bolt, the base of the ejector makes contact with the ejection plate, which pushes it forward, making it project into the striker hole. As a result of this forward movement, the cartridge pivots and is ejected downward through the ejection port.

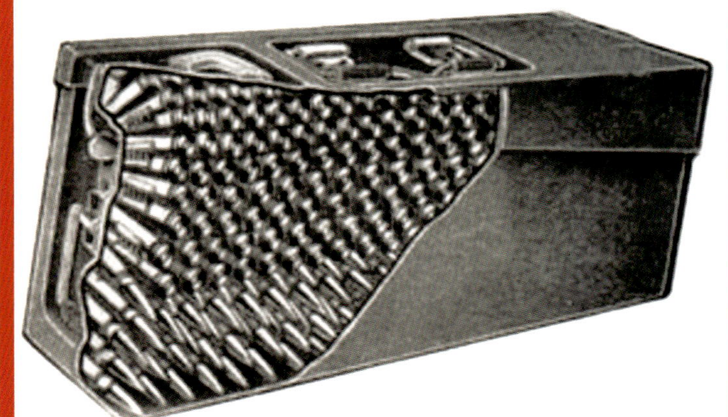

Regulation method of storing the 250-round belt in a box. The first five rows are positioned in one direction, and the next ten in the other. This makes up for the steepness of the ammunition.

Presentation of a new cartridge: During the first part of the recoil, the feed pawl slide is forced to the left. The feed pawl slips over the next round. The feed pawl slide stays in the left outermost position, where the feed pawl springs push the feed pawl down between the links of the belt.

Second phase: forward return movement of the mobile unit.

The driving force of this phase is the release of the recoil spring. As has been previously seen the release of the compensating spring, bringing back the barrel to a forward position, takes place during the first phase.

This phase has the following steps:

Introduction: The pressure exerted by the firer's finger on the trigger lowers the trigger bar by the intermediary of the sear. The bolt, thus freed from its attachment on the trigger head, inclines forward under the action of the release of the recoil spring. The bolt makes contact with the base of the cartridge presented in the magazine housing, frees it from the belt, and pushes it into the chamber by means of its spoiler. In this movement the claw of the extractor grips the base of the cartridge.

Closing: The front section of the bolt head comes into contact with the rear section of the barrel.

Locking: The body of the bolt continues on its forward movement, and the spiral ramps act on the rear locking studs of the moving bolt and impart a rotational movement toward the right. During this operation, the four rear studs on the moving

This shows a bad support position, since the man at the front should be facing his comrade and be farther away from the firing. One can only imagine the hearing damage resulting from this practice!

head position themselves in their corresponding housing at the rear of the barrel and ensure the locking of the bolt.

Firing: At the end of the movement, the pushback ramp of the firing-pin latch lifts it up. The firing pin is freed and strikes the primer on the cartridge placed in the chamber.

During the forward return of the moving part, the X-shaped housing on the rib of the feeding actuator forces it to move to the left, which leads the slide to move from the left to the right. The drive pawl pushes the second cartridge, which comes to take the place of the first and moves the belt forward. If a firing incident occurs that interrupts the sequence described above, the firer must release the trigger, cock the weapon, put it on safety before opening the cover, remove the belt or the box magazine, and check that there are no rounds in the weapon before attempting to remedy the jamming incident.

Bipod equipped with a "snowshoe" so that the MG does not sink into the snow during firing in the prone position. Note the rubber cap protecting the muzzle of the weapon, to prevent snow from entering. The man has a P. 38 holster on his belt.

MG soldier on watch. Note that the bipod is in a rear position, which gives a greater degree of angular freedom but renders the MG less stable.

The use of the MG 34 in direct fire is not excessively complex but nonetheless requires a great deal of precision and a high level of coordination between the users. Under fire, coordination can be guaranteed only by the users having undergone intensive drilling during training, so that each movement can be carried out almost as a reflex and that coordination of the crew is perfect.

After the defeat of Stalingrad, the degree of losses on the eastern front led to training gradually being reduced throughout the war. This fact, along with the rapidity of manufacture and simpler operation of the MG 42, led to the latter being adopted.

CHAPTER 4

MANUFACTURERS, PRODUCTION FIGURES, AND MARKINGS OF THE MG 34

Firing behind armored plating of a StuG III. This plating has two firing positions for the MG 34. The firer is in a high position, while the ammunition handler behind him has a metal box containing six belt drums as supplies

The beginning of mass production of the MG 34 was subject to the tightest military secrecy. This point, coupled with the destruction of records during the war, means there is a lot of uncertainty concerning the way this weapon was produced prior to 1939. The first specimens seem to have been delivered in 1936 by two enterprises: Rheinmetal-Maget and BSW.

Up to 1938, production figures were very modest. In his reference work *MG 34–MG 42: German Universal Machineguns*, Norwegian author Folke Myrvang estimates that the figure was most certainly fewer than 50,000 weapons.

This information is confirmed by the inventory of weapons of the German army carried out at the declaration of war in September 1939. It showed that the Wehrmacht had only 84,000 MG 34s at that time, out of a total of around 177,000 machine guns, the remainder being MG 08s and MG 08/15s, along with machine guns seized in countries that had already been annexed by the Reich: the Austrian MG 30 and Schwarzlose, and the Czechoslovakian ZB 26 and ZB 37.

The expansionist policy of the Third Reich was supported by democracies backing down when faced with each new territorial claim made by Germany. In addition, the annexation of a part

Code 936 of the Gustloff-Werke (ex-BSW) on a weapon made in 1940. This manufacturer was attributed with the code "dfb" at the end of that year.

Marking of the Berliner-Suhler Waffen factory (BSW) on an MG 34 made in 1937. At this time, each part was checked and stamped individually.

In 1941: Code "dfb," which is found on MG 34s made by Gustloff-Werke between 1940 and 1942, the date when manufacture of the MG 34 was stopped in the factories other than that of Brno (Brünn under German occupation). An "X" can be seen, indicating that this MG 34 was reconditioned by a Russian arsenal after the war.

Code dot of the "Waffenwerke Brünn" in occupied Czechoslovakia (at that time called "Protectorate of Bohemia-Moravia"). This factory started production of the MG 34 in 1941 and continued until the arrival of the Red Army in 1945. Small production runs were made after the war until 1953.

Reichsführer-SS Heinrich Himmler is seen testing an MG 34. Standing in the background at left is future SS general Jochem Peiper (shown here as an Untersturmführer) at the time when he was attached to Himmler's staff.

of Czechoslovakia and then Austria enabled the Wehrmacht to noticeably strengthen its arsenal by seizing military equipment and the arms industries of annexed countries. The annexation of Austria had submitted its citizens to conscription in the Wehrmacht, which also contributed to strengthen numbers.

MANUFACTURERS OF THE MG 34

During the war, a total of five companies made the MG 34: Rheinmetal, BSW, Mauser Borsigwalde, Steyr Daimler Puch, and Waffenwerke Brünn.

Rheinmetal was one of the first two makers of the MG 34; this activity was subsequently entrusted to one of its subcontractors: the Maget company.

Maget abandoned the manufacture of the MG 34 relatively quickly in favor of the MH 42. The total quantity of MG 34s produced by Rheinmetal-Maget is estimated to be 70,000.

BSW was none other than the former firm Simson & Co. As soon as the Nazis came into power, the company paid for the goodwill offered to it by the Allies when, in 1920, it was the only approved supplier of war weapons to the Reichswehr. This "collaboration" had been a cause of irritation for a good number of other makers of German weapons, fervent sympathizers of the Nazi cause.

The fact that the Simson family was of Jewish origin permitted the new power to begin a process of "Aryanization" of the company, which was expropriated and initially took the name of Berliner-Suhler Waffen- und Fahrrad-Fabrik (Arms and Cycle Factory of Berlin and Suhl), abbreviated to BSW. With the support of Gauleiter Sauckel, who at that time reigned in Thuringe, a few years later BSW was quite simply absorbed by the weapons factory of Wilhelm Gustloff, who was the director of a weapons factory at Suhl and an active militant Nazi.

Since these two first manufacturers were not sufficient to satisfy the needs caused by the war, other makers were soon engaged in the production of the MG 34.

Mauser-Werke AG (factory in Berlin/Borsigwalde). Due to production capacity at the Oberndorf factory being completely saturated by the manufacture of carbines, pistols, and field guns, Mauser organized

Weapon Markings

Manufacturer	Date of Manufacture	Manufacturer's code	No. of Waffenamt (WaA) inspector	Estimation of quantity made
Rheinmetal Maget	1937–38	Logo A	39	70,000
	1939	Logo A	11	
	1939	Logo B	11	
	1939–40	5A	11	
	1940–43	cra	11	
Waffenwerke Brünn	1940	945	63	182,000
	1941–45	dot	63	
	1948–53	*T* in a circle		70,000
Mauser Werke	1938–40	S/243	26	60,000
Borigswalde	1941–42	Ar	26	
BSW, then Gustloff	1936–39	BSW	4	130,000
	1939	G	4	
	1939–40	936	4	
	1940–43	dfb	4	
Steyr	1940–41	Bnz	623	7,000

An MG 34 and its French adversary: a model 24-29 light machine gun. ***Photo by Marc de Fromont, collection of the Royal Army Museum Brussels***

Firing position from behind an embankment with a well-protected ammunition handler

Firing from a high position from the corner of an "isba" in Belarus in 1941

a new factory in the Berlin suburb of Borsigwalde. This establishment initially made MG 34 and then K.98k carbines, and finally MG 42s at the end of the war. Mauser/Borsigwalde made around 60,000 MG 34s.

Steyr Daimler Puch AG. This important Austrian armament firm, which passed under the control of the Third Reich after the Anschluss, made MG 34 and then MG 42 as well as MP 40 and K.98k carbines. It would seem that production of the MG 34 was limited to 7,000 weapons delivered in 1941, after which the materials needed for the manufacture of the MG 34 were most likely transferred to the Brno factory (Waffenwerke Brünn), where production of this weapon could be pursued while Steyr launched mass production of the MG 42.

Waffenwerke Brünn. This large Czechoslovakian armament factory (Brünn is the German translation of Brno) started to make the MG 34 in 1941 and was the only producer to continue with manufacture until the end of the war, when it had been abandoned by other manufacturers in favor of the MG 42.

The fact that MG 34 manufacture was continued at Brno is explained by the fact the MG ball masks for tanks and fortresses could not be converted from the round-shaped MG 34 jacket to the square-shaped MG 42 jacket.

It was to respond to this particular need that the MG 34 continued to be made at Brno until 1945. This factory was the largest producer of the MG 34, since it is estimated that 182,000 weapons of this type came off its production lines.

A small series of MG 34s were made even after the war, to respond to an order from armed Jewish organizations in Palestine.

With these elements it can be concluded that a total of around 450,000 MG 34s were made during the Second World War.

From 1939 onward, the factories of the Reich produced around 5,000 examples a month. Monthly manufacture peaked at 10,170 MG 34s in April 1941.

CHAPTER 5

VARIATIONS IN PARTS MANUFACTURE OF THE MG 34

Information coming back from men using the weapon during combat, coupled with the need to simplify the manufacture of certain parts to satisfy the growing requirements in weapons, led to the development of certain parts.

PARTS DEVELOPMENT

Cover. Up until 1939, the cover of the receiver was made by being machined. These covers are identifiable by the rectangular reduction filing that appeared at their top. In the interests of increasing productivity, from 1940 onward this part was replaced by a cover in pressed metal, which was in use until the end of the war.

At the beginning of the war, some MG 34s were mounted in order to be fed with a double magazine of seventy-five rounds, quite similar but not identical to the magazine used on the MG 15 aviation machine gun. This magazine was designed to increase firing speed of weapons that used it, by freeing their mechanism from the obligation of having to move the weight of the cartridge belt.

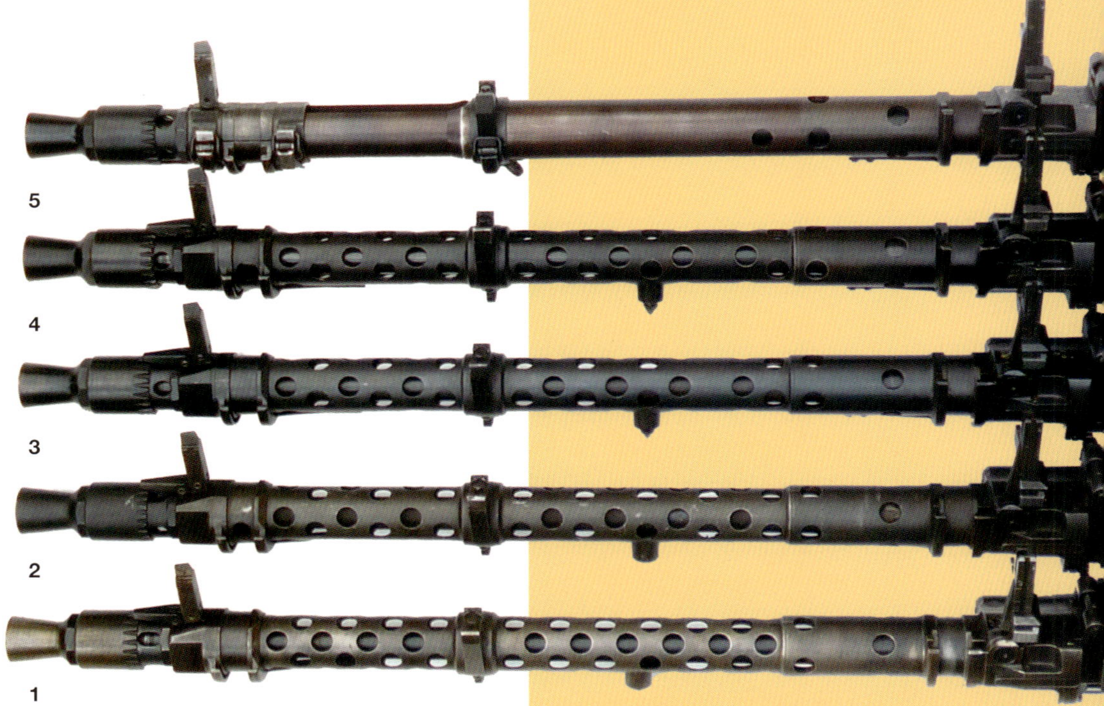

Development of the five types of cooling jackets.

From bottom to top:

1. Early-production jacket commonly known as "4 hole." The orifices are counted on a line between the bipod forward sleeve and the antiaircraft sight bracket. This version was made up to 1938 on the model of MG 13 jackets. At that period, no economy was yet required as far as machining was concerned!
2. Jacket with three orifices produced from 1939 onward. The reduction in the number of ventilation holes aimed to optimize the machining time.
3. Early-production jacket from the Brno factory (Brünn code: dot). There is another reduction in the number of ventilation holes, coupled with a lengthwise arrangement. The purpose of this modification is not easy to understand, and there is no information on the subject.
4. End-of-production "dot" jacket (from 1943); at that time, this factory was the only one producing MG 34s. The jacket is identical to the previous one but has two new ventilation holes level with the bipod forward sleeve. This addition improved the ventilation of the forward part, an area that gets hot due to the forward-backward movement of the barrel each time a shot is fired.
5. Particular 34 T jacket for the MG 34 destined for armored vehicles. This jacket, composed of high-density hardened steel, is thicker than standard jackets. This piece was very exposed on the front part of tanks, and this construction gave it an increased capacity of resistance to shrapnel. To enable its insertion into the ball mask of the armor plating, this jacket was lacking its forward sight support bracket and rear bracket, support for the antiaircraft sight. These parts were kept in a box called "MG Zubehör" and could be put into place when necessary to convert the weapon into an infantry machine gun. This version is wrongly called "heavy-barreled MG 34." In reality, only the cooling jacket is different. Its thickness and the type of steel used make it heavier than the standard perforated version (the barrel is standard format).

In the background, the knurled adjusting knob of the first type of bipod, compared to the second, more common type

Comparison of the recoil booster cylinders. *Bottom*: an early version with oblong holes; *top*: the second model, with round holes. This development simplified the machining process.

The photos of the period do indeed often show this magazine placed on MG 34s used as antiaircraft weapons. When the twinned MG 34, then MG 42, entered into service, the use of the seventy-five-round magazine fell into disuse, and they are a rare sight on photos taken at the end of the war.

Barrel jacket. The perforated jacket surrounding the barrel has a number of orifices, designed as much to facilitate the circulation of air to cool the barrel as to make the part lighter. In its initial version (version 1), the jacket was simply made based on that of the MG 13 (distribution between holes). The first jackets are identifiable by the presence of four holes between the antiaircraft sight support and the foresight support, whereas subsequent versions have only three. With time, the number of orifices was reduced to render the jacket more robust (version 2). For the same reason, later on, a different arrangement of the holes was tried (version 3). The MG 34s mounted on armored vehicles were equipped with a thicker jacket on which two large slits at the end of the jacket ensured cooling. We will come back to machine guns destined for panzers later on.

Two cooling jackets with differences in the bipod feed rail. From 1943 onward, the Brünn workshop machined two holes at 180 degrees at this point. It was the only factory to make this development.

Gas ports on the muzzle. The gas ports positioned behind the booster cone were initially oblong; they later became circular.

All these developments had the primary objective of optimizing production of this weapon; to reduce production time and cost and to make its operation more reliable:

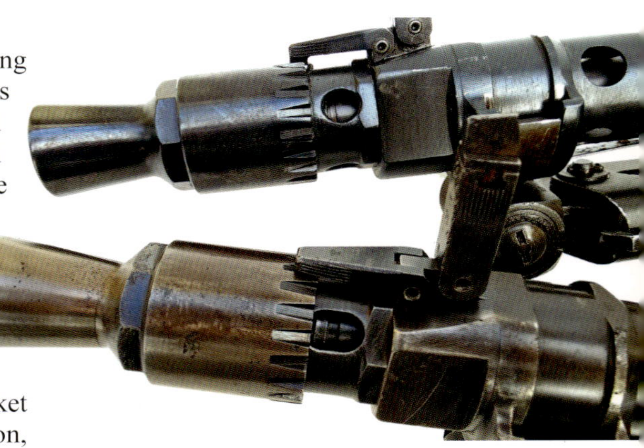

Magazine housing. In its ordinary version the MG 34 was belt fed, introduced from the left side of the receiver. Some MG 34s were sometimes modified to be fed from the right, so they could be used on a twin mount (fed from the left for the "left" MG 34, and from the right for the "right" MG 34), or, when the environment of the weapon prevented an easy feeding, from the left (in turrets of tanks and certain fortified positions, for example).

Beautiful propaganda photo showing a Croat solider (recognizable by the badge on his chest pocket) with an MG 34 on his shoulder, belt around his neck, and grenade in his belt

The two versions of the bipod "fixing stud" in folded position under the cooling jacket. *Top*: The early version descended from the model of the MG 13. *Bottom*: The second model.

Three of the main types of bipod. *From top to bottom*, the first type of MG 13; the midproduction model, on which the retaining clip was replaced by spring bolts; and the end-of-production model, which no longer has the height-adjusting knob.

Development of grips and receivers.

Right: The early version with machining in the body of the receiver and the pin for housing the button for controlling firing speed, which was just rear of the trigger guard. The large screw on the base of the grip maintained the cyclic rate reducer in the grip.

Middle: The transitional version on an MG from 1940, with a new version of grip but still with the early, machined receiver. This probably came from a remainder of stock of the previous version.

Left: The definitive version, without the specific machining for the firing-speed regulation control in the body of the receiver.

Four main variants of magazine housing were made:

- The first variant had no protruding ears for fixing of the *Trommel* (belt drum) or the pierced clip that fixed on the top cover pin. This model is reversible so it can be used with a belt fed from the right.
- The second had protruding ears for fixing the *Trommel*, containing a belt of fifty cartridges and the pierced clip to be able to pivot with the cover
- The third has a small bracket at the end of the feed tray, acting as a belt stop destined to hold the engaged belt in place when the firer opens the top cover. The first version of bracket was a single part fixed by two rivets. This appendage was initially added on the housing by unit armorers (*Waffenmeisterm*).
- The fourth is identical, but the belt catch is no longer added but directly pressed in the part used to make the magazine housing.

Bipod and its support. There are three main variants:

- The first, which is quite simply an MG 13 bipod, has a hinged flap that was used to keep the two parts of the bipod together during transport.
- The second does not have this flap but is fitted with spring bolts.
- The third no longer has a screw to adjust height.

Four versions of buttstock. The first versions were made in wood, then the Bakelite version appeared with steel reinforcement braces, and then these braces disappeared. *Bottom left*: A version in Bakelite with no numbering, containing more wood shavings in the phenolic resin.

Very fine early buttstock in wood made by BSW in 1935, with the stamps of the Reichswehr and the Nazi eagle together. *MRA*

First type of firing pin nut on the left, second type on the right

Top: Two models of the first type. *Left*: Early type in its original state, and on the right a modified version with a cut-and-belt bent hook.
This first version was reversible, meaning it was fed from the left (normal) or from the right by turning the feed tray on the receiver 180° (it was necessary to change other parts in order to be fed from the right).
Bottom: Three models of the second type. *From the left*: An early-type second model (1940); *in the middle*, a transition model modified by the unit armorer, who added the cut-and-belt bent hook; and, last, the final version.

The stud, on which the bipod is bolted when it is folded under the weapon, was a rounded shape on the MG 13 and on all the first MG 34s. It subsequently took on a pointed shape, which facilitated the insertion of the bipod flaps.

Some MG 34s made after 1945 in Brno (code: "dot") for the state of Israel were fitted with a Czech ZB 26 light machine gun bipod mounted on the sleeve of the jacket by means of an adaptor.

Pistol grip. The specifications established by the Reichswehr initially planned that the future machine gun of the German army should be adjusted for two firing speeds: the first, around 700 shots per minute (normal firing speed); the second, slightly higher at 1,000 shots per minute (antiaircraft firing speed).

This capability was on the very first MG 34, thanks to a firing-speed regulator (*Regler*) mounted on the inside of the grip. The desired firing speed was selected by a lever positioned at the top of the left plate to the position "L" (*Langsam* = slow) or "S" (*Schnell* = fast).

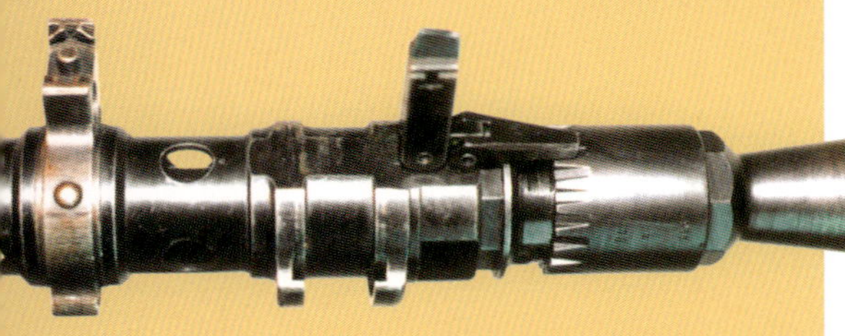

MG 34S jacket

This selector does not seem to have been satisfactory, since it was very rapidly removed and the corresponding parts were removed from weapons that had been fitted with them.

The grips used with a firing-speed regulator are identifiable from the exterior by the button situated between the trigger and the grip plates and on the interior of the housing that held the regulation mechanism. The receivers of weapons equipped with this type of grip have empty housings, which were originally destined to receive the parts of the trigger related to the adjustable-firing-speed system.

It should be noted that the grip plates were made in a cast black Bakelite from the beginning to the end of the war. Some MG 34s with aluminum grip plates can be encountered, but these are likely to be replacements made in postwar Czechoslovakia in a lighter and less fragile material than Bakelite, the supply of which was then no longer limited, unlike during the war.

Safety lever. A new type of safety lever was adopted in July 1938.

Buttstock. Initially made in walnut, the buttstock was then made in Bakelite. This material was quite sensitive to impact, so some buttstocks had metallic braces at the upper and lower corners of the butt plate.

Comparison between an MG 34S and a standard MG 34. Very few internal or external parts are interchangeable between these two models.

MG 34P jacket with its two brackets, so as to be able to use this version destined for the Panzers in an infantry version

The contents of the "MG-Zubehör" box: a bipod, a buttstock, a carrying strap, and the two jacket brackets

At the end of the war, the chemical products necessary for the production of Bakelite were restricted, so in February 1943 it was decided to abandon the buttstocks in Bakelite and go back to those in wood, this time in beech.

Moving bolt. There are two variants in the shape of the firing-pin nut. The first version was made with a notched locking piece, which was not easy to handle or make. The second version was with a flap foldable to an angle of 90° for the purpose of unlocking.

UNUSUAL VERSIONS OF THE MG 34

The MG 34P: The MG 13 and then the MG 34 machine guns were the only weapons of type Pzwl Ausf.A armored vehicles at the beginning of the war. The similarity between the jackets on the barrels of the two machine guns meant the MG 13 could easily be replaced by the MG 34 when this new model was adopted.

Subsequently, the machine guns gradually left their place to ever-more-powerful guns but nonetheless continued to be mounted in the hull and turret of various armored vehicles as close-quarter defense weapons against enemy infantry.

The mounting on an armored ball mask on the interior of the hull of the vehicle left a good portion of the jacket exposed outside the armor, where the fragile jacket was at the mercy of enemy shrapnel.

Specific bracket for locking the 34T flash suppressor

MG 34 mounted on a StuG assault gun; the firer is protected by a shield.

The MG 34P in its "smooth" configuration for insertion in a panzer ball mask

The "MG-Zubehör" onboard box (accessories for MG) containing the kit to transform it to an infantry version. The Gurtkasten 34 was destined for Sd.Kfz. 222 armored vehicles.

Parachutists using an MG 34 mounted on a Lafette fitted with leather-covered pads

Machine-made top cover for the Patronentrommel 34, showing the dust flaps in closed position

Top cover with the marking specific to the contract of the MG 34 delivered to Portugal

To avoid the machine guns mounted on armored vehicles being put out of action too frequently, in February 1941 the Wehrmacht adopted a thick jacket in tempered steel for the MG 34 of the Panzertruppen. These had only a few perforations and were called *Panzermantel* (armored jacket or jacket for armored vehicles).

Each armored vehicle received an MG 34 with one of these specific jackets and was also supplied with a small metal box containing the required accessories (buttstock, bipod, foresight and its support, support for antiaircraft firing sight, and sling) for transforming the tank-mounted machine gun to a land-firing one. The transformation had to deal with the absence of the bipod-fixing stud under the heavy barrel jacket.

This explains the fact that sometimes MG 34s with a jacket for armored vehicles fitted with a fixing stud are encountered. This part was added in unit by brazing. This modification renders the reintroduction with ball mask impossible. It is, however, possible that this modification was made after the war.

MG 34/41 or MG 34 S: This is a version of the MG 34, developed at Rheinmetal by Louis Stange, designed to have a faster firing speed. The result was obtained by using a shorter barrel (500 mm) that was also therefore lighter, as well as a more powerful recoil spring and a recoil booster with larger openings. Only several hundred MG 34-41s were evaluated, since this project was interrupted by the MG 42 entering into service. The MG 34-41 is sometimes called MG 34S (S for *Schnell*).

In 1943, Germany delivered a batch of MG 34s to Portugal. In the Portuguese army the MG 34 is called "Metralhadora m/944." It would appear that 1,000 MG 34s were sent to Portugal in two deliveries of 400 and 600 weapons, accompanied by 334 Lafette 34–type tripod mounts, with an undetermined number of MGZ34 optics and various accessories.

Apart from the identification stamped on the top cover, "Konstruktion Rheinmetal-Borsig" with the contract number, these MG 34s are also identifiable by the letters A (*automatico*) and T (*tiro a tiro*) on the trigger, identifying, respectively, the automatic firing position and single-shot fire.

This midwar MG 34 is next to a transport case for a spare barrel and some aiming stakes used for indirect fire. At the top of the photo, there is a rack for the transport of two drums and a gunner tool pouch. *Photo by Marc de Fromont, Royal Army Museum Collection, Brussels*

CHAPTER 6

THE MG 42 MACHINE GUN

Armed coastal position with an MG 42 on its Lafette, weighted by two ammunition boxes on either side. The MG 42 is of the first type, recognizable by its "fixing stud" for attaching the bipod when it was folded.

In 1936, a four-year plan was adopted to prepare the German economy and industry for the war that the Nazis considered would break out between 1940 and 1943. A competition was opened to German industrialists to find a replacement for the MG 34. The new weapon had to be easy to make and to use pressed metal if possible. It also had to use the same belts as the MG 34 and have the maximum number of accessories in common with it.

The retained prototype was presented to the military authorities in October 1937 by the Paul Kurt Johannes Grossfuss Metall- und Lackier-Warenfabrik company of Döbeln in Saxe. The fact that this enterprise, until then not involved in the manufacture of weapons, was successful while Rheinmetal Borsig had its project ruled out was proof that the traditional armorers could be abandoned in favor of productivity.

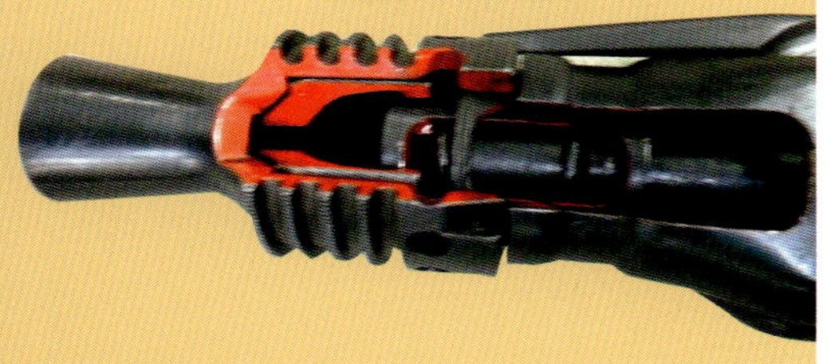

Recoil booster and the end of the barrel

This development in the German armaments industry reached its peak in 1942, when the whole of the industry of the Reich passed under the control of the Ministry of Armaments, led by Albert Speer.

The weapon, conceived by Dr. Gruner, kept the principle of short recoil of the barrel and locking of the bolt head in a part solid with the rear of the barrel, already in use on the MG 34. On the other hand, the Grossfuss machine gun was made up of a receiver made of two half pieces of stamped sheet metal, and the locking of the bolt was no longer operated by rotation as on the MG 34, but by the separation of the two cylindrical rollers positioned on either side of the bolt head.

This locking principle is found in various forms on several weapons developed at a later date.

Starting in 1938, when the Grossfuss machine gun was the only one in the running as a designated

MG 42 used for training, with windows cut out so the main parts of the active mechanism can be observed

Foreground: The recoil spring of the barrel. *Rear*: That of the bolt.

Shock absorber and buttstock spring-loaded buffer catch

replacement of the MG 34, it was further improved by the addition of a system for the rapid change of the barrel, which was far better than that on the MG 34 and still remains today one of the best systems of its type.

After an experimentation phase of various preproduction models in combat units, which took place between 1939 and 1942, the weapon considered as ready was adopted during 1942 under the name "MG 42." Production of the new weapon started immediately at Grossfuss, but also at Maget in Berlin, before being launched in other factories.

Principal Characteristics	
Caliber	7.92 × 57 mm (7.92 Mauser)
Feeding	Soft, not detachable metal bands of 50 or 250 rounds
Total length	122 cm
Weight (with no ammunition)	11.6 kg with bipod
Barrel length	56.5 cm (4 grooves on right)
Weight of tripod mount	19.5 kg
Single barrel weight	1.8 kg
Barrel change in sustained fire	approx. every 200 rounds or every 400 rounds maximum

PRESENTATION

As with the MG 34, the MG 42 belonged to a category of general-purpose machine guns, called such because they could be used as a light infantry machine gun on a bipod, or as a heavy machine gun when placed on a tripod mount. They could also be used as fortress-mounted weapons or weapons onboard vehicles.

In the last two configurations, the MG 42 was reserved for exterior mounts. For setting up under a gun turret, its system of barrel change required that the right side of the receiver remain free; thus the MG 34 was often the preferred weapon in this situation until the end of the war.

The MG 42 was conceived for firing against both land and air targets. It is equipped with a lateral system allowing for rapid change of the barrel. It is fed by the same flexible metal belts with nondetachable links as the MG 34. The belts usually used had 250 and 50 rounds.

The configuration of the links at the extremities of the belt meant that one belt could be easily connected to another or to a belt tab. It could be used only for continuous-burst fire. Its firing speed was very high (theoretical rate of fire: between 1,200 and 1,500 shots per minute).

An MG 42 with raised cover, its *Trommel*, and its barrel carrier, along with the gunner tool pouch, showing its contents. This pouch is of the last type in Presstoff and is marked with the code "fuq" 1945.

The main parts of the weapon include the following:

1. The frame (or receiver), which is made in sheet metal, folded and welded.

Only several zones of contact with other parts of the mechanism were rectified. The right side of the receiver is largely open to allow the barrel to be extracted easily. There is a cylindrical-shaped barrel guide sleeve on the inside of the front end of the frame, one side of which is indented. This configuration is indispensable given that the barrel must be able to carry out lengthwise movements during fire, as well as lateral movements when it is being replaced. This band transmits the thrust of the gas trapped in the recoil booster system to the barrel.

A double-purpose part is screwed on at the muzzle of the weapon:

- Its rear part is made of a gas expansion chamber, with the edges pierced with a dozen circular orifices, which contains a cylindrical-conical part on which the pressure of gas leaving the barrel acts. This unit constitutes the recoil booster system bearing six slots.

- The forward part is a simple conical-shaped flash hider.

DISASSEMBLY FOR RAPID FIELD MAINTENANCE

Open cover with the feed tray in a vertical position.

While keeping the top cover and the feed tray at a 90-degree angle, with its flat spot facing forward, pull the top cover bolt out on the left. The top cover and feed tray may now be removed.

Hold the buttstock catch down and twist the buttstock a quarter turn.

Hold down the bolt on the buffer and turn it a quarter turn to extract it from the frame with the bolt spring. The bolt can then be slid rearward.

Move the bolt back and extract it from the frame. Noting how it comes out of its housing at this point will make reassembly easier.

Extract the bipod from the frame by pressing the latch forward.

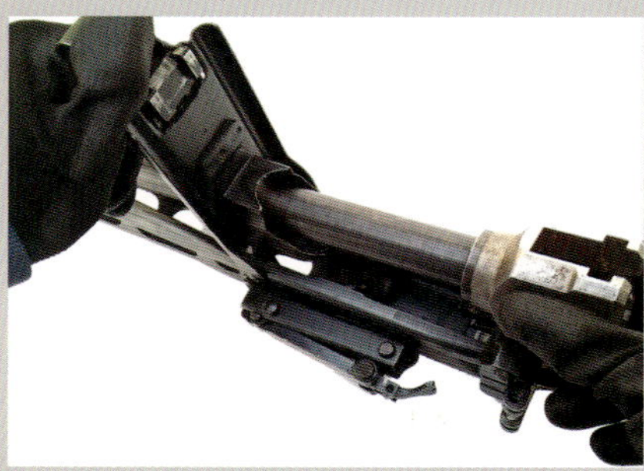

Remove the barrel, then open the barrel change latch 90 degrees.

Unscrew the flash hider and its recoil booster, then move the top catch upward.

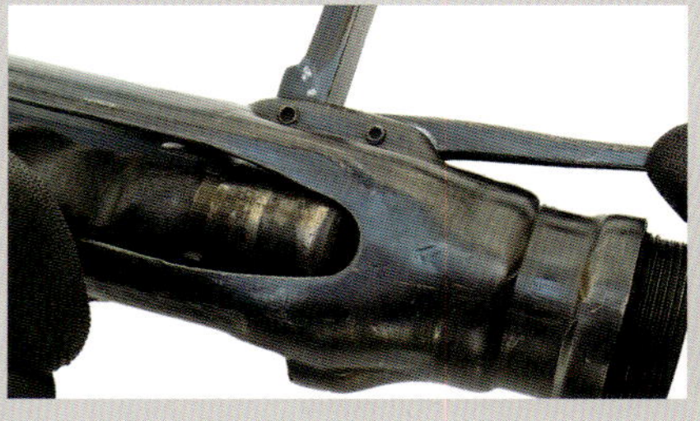

Remove the barrel guide by sliding a finger in the cavity while lifting the flash-hider catch. Extract it from the frame by the opening under the rear sight.

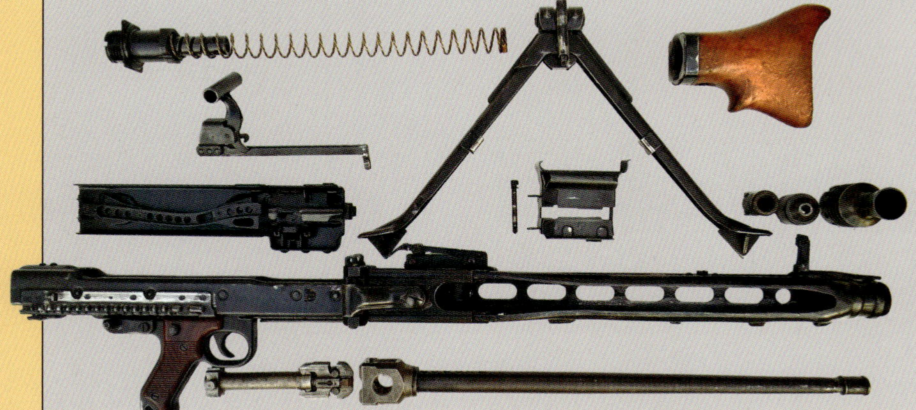

The principal elements are now disassembled, and rapid field maintenance can be carried out.

MG 34 and MG 42 machine guns. Also in this photo: a double spare-barrel carrier, a transport case for stick grenades, two drum transport cases and a P.38 pistol with its second-model holster. *Photo by Marc de Fromont, Royal Army Museum Collection, Brussels*

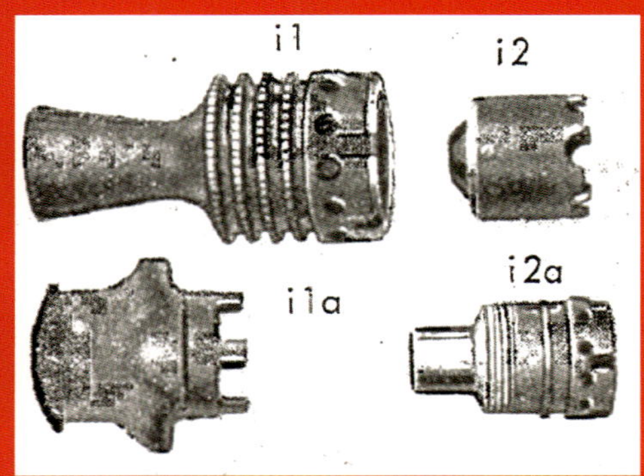

Comparison of a standard flash hider and an experimental one tested in several units. It was not retained because the users complained it made a very unpleasant sound.

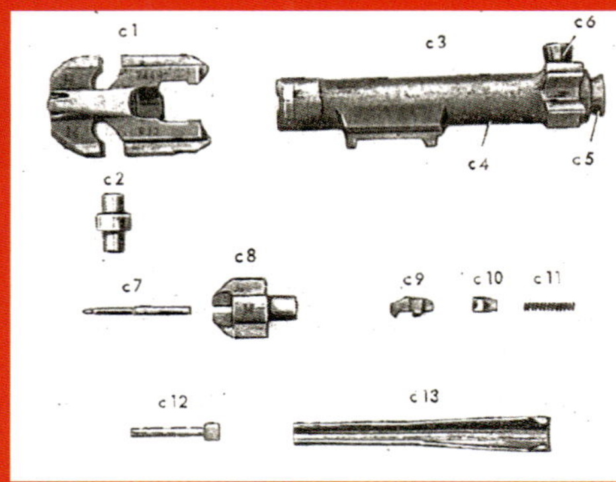

Bolt of a disassembled MG 42. The simplification is striking compared to that of the MG 34.

Fallschirmjäger **in Russia, heavily laden with ammunition and with a first type 42 (see the cocking handle, bipod, and buttstock in Bakelite) on his shoulder.** ***BA***

Other noteworthy elements of the frame are the following:

- On the right side, the guideway in which the cocking handle slides
- At its lower part, the ejection port, which can be sealed by a moveable spring flap for transport and opens automatically when there is any movement of the bolt
- The assembly of the bipod on a circular guideway, which was used on the MG 13, MG 34, and even versions of the MG 15 transformed for land use, had to be abandoned on the MG 42 where the frame had a square rather than a circular section. Under the forward part of the frame, two appendages obtained by stamping allow the bipod of choice to be fixed, in forward or rear position. They can also be used for setting up the weapon on certain types of mounts.
- The barrel change flap is found on the right side of the forward part.

On the upper part:

- The hinge linking the two parts of the magazine housing to the frame
- The foldable notch sight, calibrated from 200 to 2,000 meters in 100-meter graduations, with the left side of the base of the sight, a sight bracket for antiaircraft fire
- A little farther near the forward part is a base for fixing a sight for antiaircraft fire, quite similar to but not interchangeable with the models used on the MG 13 and MG 34.
- At the front of the receiver is the foldable foresight and the flash-hider catch.

2. The cover, articulated with the frame by a pin placed at its forward part; this has a spring-loaded catch at its rear part. On the inside there a hollow feed lever placed at the halfway point on the inside of the cover, which slides the feed lever stud positioned at the top of the body of the bolt. The function of this feed lever arm is to transform the forward-to-rear movement of the moving bolt into a lateral movement designed to move the ammunition belt forward.

The feed slide assembly consists of a lever that has two arms with cartridge pawls attached. One arm holds the front- and rear-feed pawls, and the other holds the middle double-feed pawls. The feed slide assembly slides back and forth on the feed slide assembly bolt. The feeding ramp in which the ammunition belt slides is under the cover and articulated on the same axis.

3. The pistol grip has the trigger mechanism (continuous-burst fire only) and the safety catch. The forward part of the pistol grip fits in a notch in the frame, whereas the rear part is held in place by a pin. The grip has striated grip plates on both sides in Bakelite (vegetable fibers bonded in a phenolic resin, in a red, brown, or black color).

4. The barrel is composed of a conical-cylindrical tube, the rear of which is tightly screwed in a part with flat sides: the locking piece of the barrel, in which the bolt head is locked.

5. The moving bolt is composed of two main parts:

- the head, which carries the extractor and the locking rollers
- the body, which contains the firing pin, the firing-pin support, and the ejector; on the upper part, the body of the bolt has the "feed lever stud," which engages in the feed lever on the inside of the cover

Only the head of the bolt is machined. The body is rough cast and only the contact zones are rectified: cocking-handle notch, sear notch.

6. The recoil spring is composed of two twisting wires, brazed at the extremities.

7. The buffer consists of a solid spring serving as a hold-open latch for the bolt during its recoil movement. The rear of the buffer is fixed to the buttstock. The buffer/frame and the buttstock/buffer units were made by screws with interrupted threads, where each one is blocked in position by a stop.

8. The buttstock is short and solid, as on the MG 34; the buttstock on the MG was made in Bakelite in the first versions and then in wood.

Simultaneous fire of a 34 and a 42 at short distance, judging by the positions of the sights.

9. The bipod. On the MG 42 the bipod is equipped with a simple catch in a housing placed under the frame and made of pressed metal. As on the MG 13 and 34, there are two fixing points, allowing the bipod to be mounted either in forward or rear position. In reality, the photos of the period show that the bipod was more often used in the forward position. The rear housing, nearer to the machine gun's center of gravity, was used more to set up the weapon on various mounts (antiaircraft tripods and vehicle mounts).

A magnificent 1942 early-type MG 42. This one still has the first-type Bakelite buttstock and bipod.

CHAPTER 7

USE AND OPERATION OF THE MG 42

The mechanism of the MG 42, and particularly its bolt locking system operated by locking rollers, inspired many other postwar weapons designers, and it is still being used on many current variants of this weapon.

Muzzles of barrels on the MG 34 (*top*) and the MG 42 (*bottom*)

Feeding: The user moves the cocking handle to the rear until the bolt locks on the sear. Then the cocking handle must be pushed forward until locking. After putting the weapon on safety by pushing the safety catch above the grip on the left (the letter "S" then appears at the rear of the catch), he engages a belt from the left side of the weapon following the procedure previously described for the MG 34.

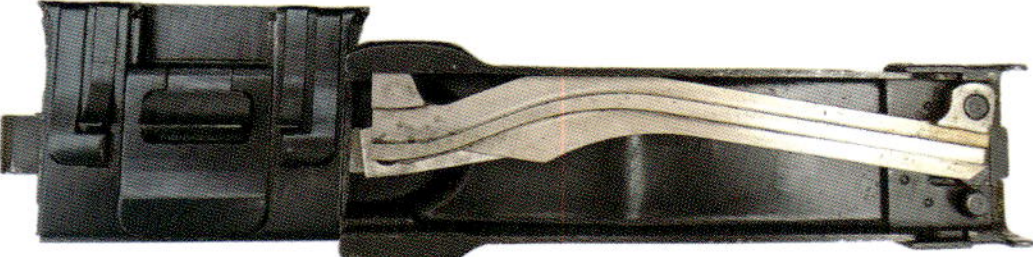

Feeding mechanisms under the cover: MG 42 (*top*), MG 34 (*bottom*). The relationship is clear in spite of the clear differences.

The first cartridge of the belt is now in contact with the feed tray stop cleat; the firer must close the cover and check that the feed lever is well positioned opposite the bolt feed lever stud.

At this moment, the first cartridge of the belt is held in position

- on the right by the feed ramp stop,
- from underneath by the distribution lips on the feed tray, and
- at the top by the inserting ramp, and on the left by a ratchet.

To fire, the safety must be put on "fire" position by pushing it to the right (the letter "F" is then visible on the rear side of the button); then press the trigger.

At that moment, the movement of the sear frees the moving bolt, which is projected forward

Trench defended by two MG 42s and an MG 34

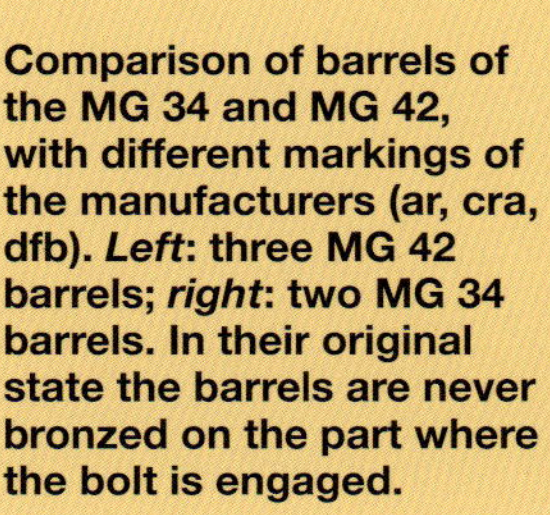

Comparison of barrels of the MG 34 and MG 42, with different markings of the manufacturers (ar, cra, dfb). *Left*: three MG 42 barrels; *right*: two MG 34 barrels. In their original state the barrels are never bronzed on the part where the bolt is engaged.

The first MG 42s put into service were used in North Africa with the Afrikakorps, as brought to life by this photo. ***Photo by Marc de Fromont, Royal Army Museum Collection, Brussels***

by its recoil spring. As it moves, the bolt has contact with the base of the cartridge in presentation position and pushes it forward. The tip of the bullet slides on the inserting ramp of the cover, then on the bevel of the chamber, thus guiding the cartridge in the chamber.

At the same time, the cocking-handle notch, positioned at the top of the body of the bolt, forces the feed lever to move from right to left, causing the cartridge pawls of the belt to move from left to right, which moves the belt forward, until the second cartridge on the belt takes its place on the inserting ramp.

Locking, firing: While the bolt continues its forward movement, the two locking rollers positioned on either side of the bolt head press on the ramps carried by the receiver. Under the pressure of the bolt, the rollers move to the exterior and take their place in the housings corresponding to the barrel-locking piece. The bolt is now locked to the barrel.

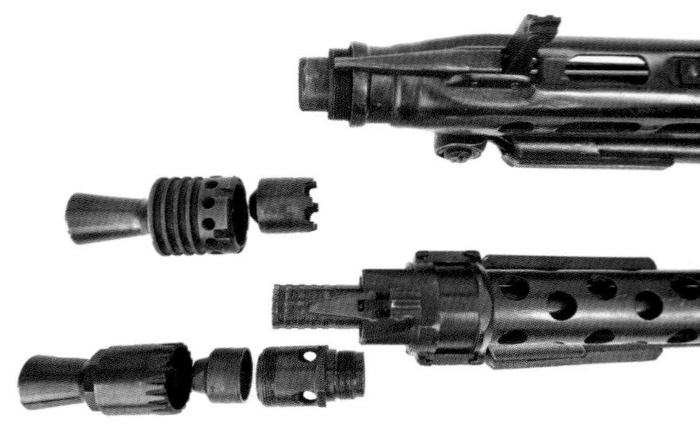

Recoil booster of the MG 42 (*top*) and the MG 34 (*bottom*)

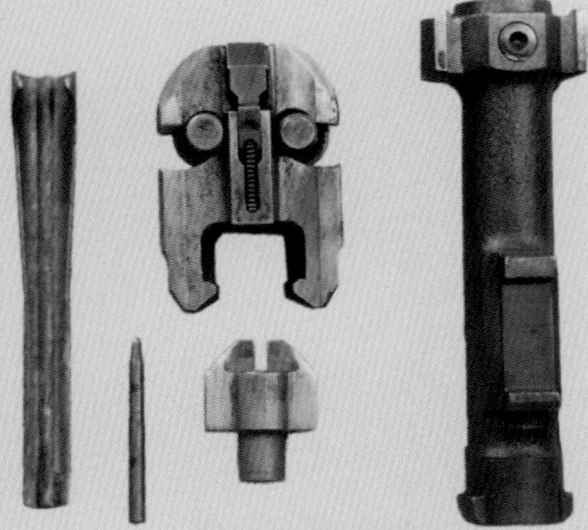

MG 42 bolt after rudimentary disassembly

Two grenadiers of the 23rd SS Division "Nederland" carrying out maintenance on an MG 42 and its Lafette

Engagement of the first link on the belt on the cut-and-belt bent hook on the feed tray

The bolt carrier then pushes the firing pin forward. The tip of the firing pin protrudes into the striker hole and strikes the primer on the cartridge in the chamber, which causes firing (which is possible only after the complete locking of the bolt to the barrel).

Barrel recoil: when the projectile comes out of the muzzle of the barrel, the gases that propel it exert a pressure on the forward section of the barrel by the intermediary of the recoil booster.

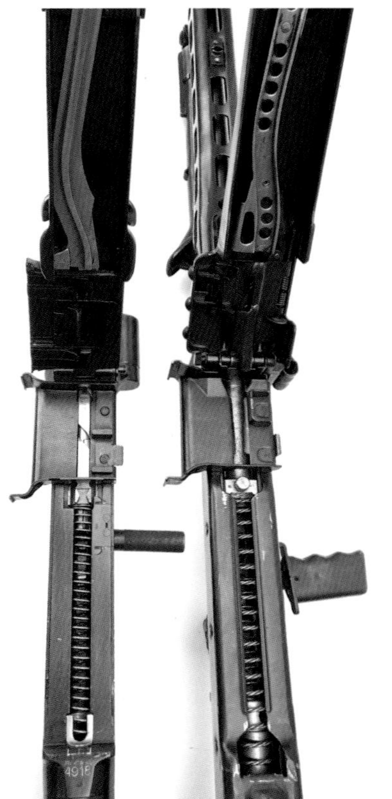

Comparison of the internal arrangement with open covers (the grip on the model on the left is a copy)

Feeding via a *Trommel* fixed to its feeding tray. The first link is attached to the cut-and-belt bent hook.

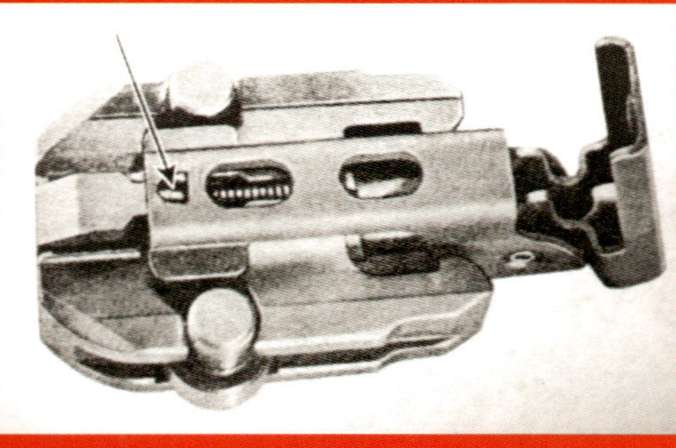
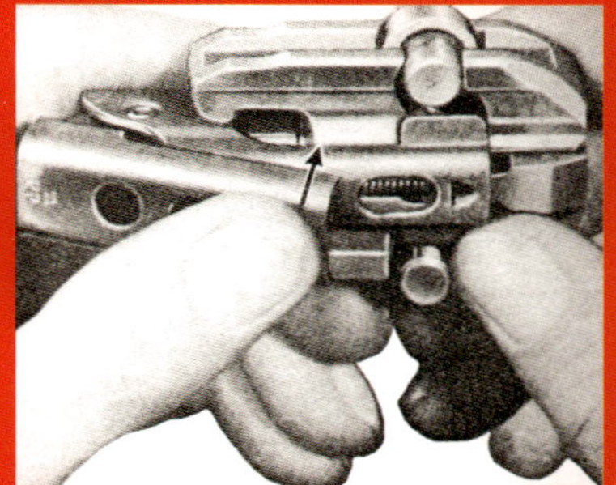
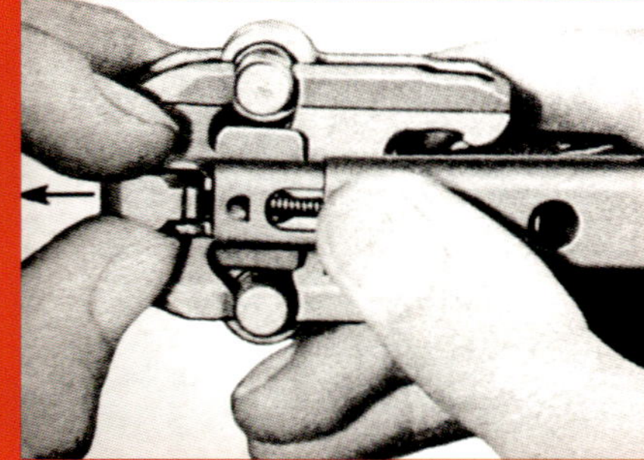

Method of disassembling the extractor from the bolt head

This phenomenon acts in synergy with the pressure exerted on the bolt striker hole by the base of the casing, when the shot is fired, causing the recoil of the barrel-bolt unit over a length of about 12 mm.

Unlocking: After a short recoil of the barrel-bolt unit, the recoil of the barrel is stopped by a thrust stop. Under the effect of the pressure exerted on the bolt by the base of the cartridge that has just been fired, the bolt continues to be subject to a recoil movement. As the barrel and bolt continue recoiling, the large-diameter portions of the bolt rollers hit the unlocking ramps on the camming piece. The bolt, now unlocked, continues its recoil, whereas the barrel is brought back to its initial position by a spring ("barrel recoil spring") positioned at the inside of the receiver on the left side.

Extraction, case ejection: By following its recoil, the bolt ensures the extraction of the case. During this recoil movement of the bolt, the stud placed at its upper side slides in the feed lever in the inside of the cover of the weapon. The function of this guideway is to transform the longitudinal movement of the bolt into a transversal movement to allow the cartridge belt to run from left to right, until the next cartridge in the belt is in contact with the stop cleat in the presentation position. After going as far to the rear as possible, the rear section of the bolt, in which the ejector is housed, hits the buffer. The ejector is then pushed forward and swings the empty case downward through the ejection port.

Loading a new cartridge and firing: The bolt then goes forward again under the action of its recoil spring. During this movement, it has contact with the base of the cartridge being presented and is then led forward, extracting it from the belt. Pushed forward by the bolt head and downward by the cartridge push, the cartridge is introduced in the chamber. Meanwhile, led by the feed lever, the rod catch makes another half movement. The bolt locks to the barrel, and the firing pin strikes the primer of the cartridge that has just been loaded.

This cycle repeats itself as long as the weapon is loaded and the firer presses the trigger, except of course if there is some kind of firing incident that affects the operation of the machine gun.

An MG 34P mounted on the turret of a panzer. The bag for the belt is clearly visible.

CHAPTER 8

MARKINGS AND FINISHES OF THE MG 42

Marking "bnz" for the manufacturer Steyr

MARKINGS ON THE RECEIVER

The manufacture of the MG 42 made a substantial use of parts made by subcontractors in factories dispersed throughout Germany, which rendered the process of production less vulnerable to the Allied strategic-bombing campaign. The identity of the factory that did the final assembly appeared at the rear of the receiver, on the left side in the form of a two- or three-letter code.

The following appeared above the manufacturer's code:

- The date, written in full from 1942 to 1943, then later a coded date in the form of two capital letters
- From 1942 to 1943, the identification of the model: "MG 42"
- The serial number, composed of one to four figures, followed (or not) by a small letter. This number appears in this place only in theory.
- A code composed of two or three letters, which is the "main manufacturer"; in other words, the one who carried out the final assembly of parts made either by itself or subcontractors, the latter having their own identification code. There were four "main manufacturers":

Maget
Gustloff
Mauser Borsigwalde
Steyr

Weapon Markings

Manufacturer	Date of manufacture	Code	Code date	Waffenamt (WaA)	Estimate of quantity manufactured
Maget	1942	bpr	1942	47	165,000
	1942	cra	1942	47 or 11	
	1943	cra	1943	11	
	1943	cra	GH	11	
	1944	cra	NC	11	
	1945	swd	NC	11	
Gustloff	1943	dfb	1943	4	105,000
	1943	dfb	FG	4	
	1944	dfb	MU	4	
	1945	svq	SM	4	
Mauser	1943	ar	1943	26	54,000
	1943	ar	JT	26	
	1944	ar	DF	26	
	1945	dd	DF	26	
Steyr	1942	1942	bnz	623	69,000
	1943	1943	bnz	623	
	1943	GZ	bnz	623	
	1944	PJ	bnz	623	
	1944	PJ	swj	623	
	1945	XE	swj	623	

It would seem that Grossfuss never carried out the final assembly of the MG 42 apart from several 1942 preproduction specimens with the code "bpr." However, the company supplied frames, covers, and various other components identifiable by the "bpr" marking to Maget and Mauser.

The majority of the MG 42 with the marking of one of these two manufacturers are assembled with Grossfuss receivers.

Steyr made the majority of components contained in the weapon, whereas the MG 42 assembled by Gustloff generally used frames marked "arz."

The "dd" marking for Mauser; the initials "DF" indicate the year of manufacture as 1945.

The "cra" marking for Maget; NC = 1944 to 1945

VARIOUS MARKINGS

As the end of the war approached, Germany was subjected to ever more intensive aerial bombing. After the Allied landings in Italy and France, the factories in the eastern part of the Reich, which at the beginning of the war were beyond the range of Allied aviation, were increasingly subjected to attacks by heavy Anglo-American bombers, since they were now able to operate from the Continent. Later, the Soviet advance also disrupted production.

In addition, the principle of subcontracting out the manufacture of secondary parts, already carried out at the beginning of the war, spread to more and more components of the weapon. This explains the diverse manufacturer's codes on constituent parts of the same weapon.

It is highly likely that some subcontractors supplied several factories carrying out the final assembly of the MG 42; this is proved by the presence of secondary parts having the same code on MGs bearing markings of different manufacturers. Apart from the Waffenamt inspection stamps (eagle on a number sometimes preceded by the letters "WaA"), there are some parts that have isolated letters, most likely corresponding to inspections of certain stages in production.

After 1945, with a production of MG 42s estimated at around 400,000 between 1942 and May 1945, a considerable part of which were captured by the Red Army, the communist countries had sufficient stocks to supply the movements called "liberation," without having to restart production. Otherwise, the production lines situated

MG 42 mounted on a Volkswagen Schwimmwagen amphibious vehicle

Buttstocks, buffers, and springs of the MG 34 (*top*) and 42 (*bottom*)

The "svq" marking for the manufacturer Gustloff-Werke; SM = 1945

The "cra" marking for Maget; GH = 1943

New code "swd" assigned to Maget at the end of the war; the letters NC indicate the year 1945.

Code "cra" for the Maget factory; the year was indicated in full until the beginning of 1943.

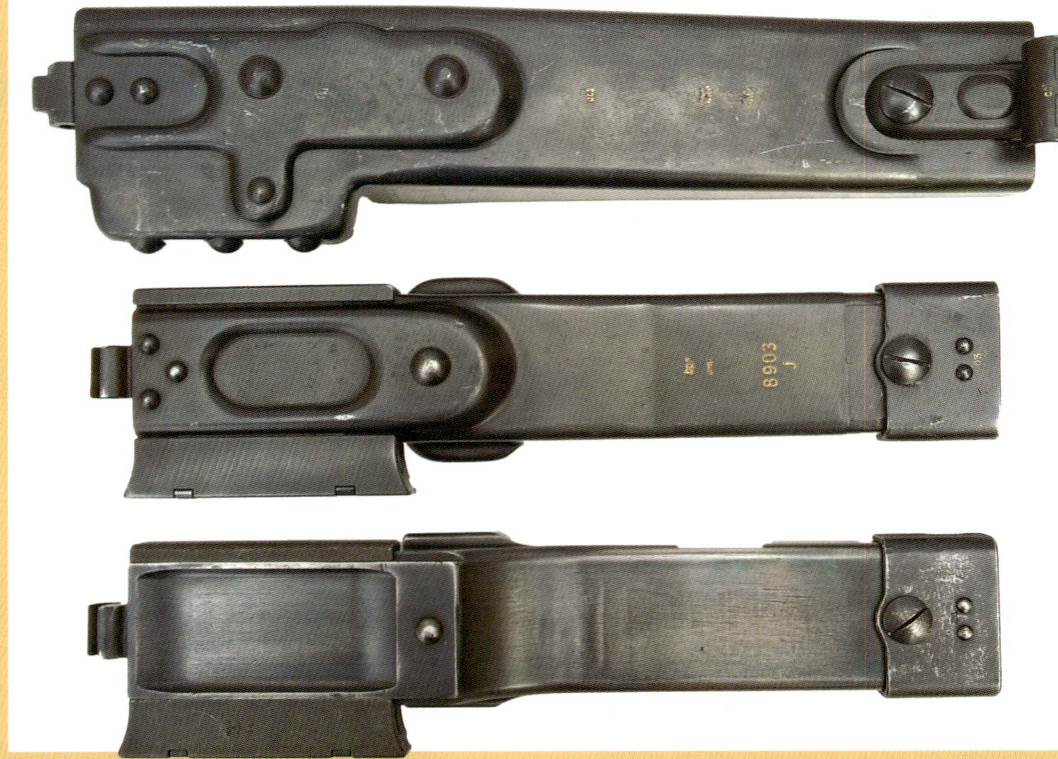

From bottom to top: the machined top cover of the MG 34 in its first version, then the stamped version, then, *at the top*, the more solid version of the MG 42

Panzergrenadier with an MG 42 over his shoulder during the attack of the Ardennes. He has a tool kit on his belt with the asbestos hot-barrel pad placed under the flap.

Close-up of the bases of the fixation points for the antiaircraft ring sights on the MG 34 (*left*) and 42 (*right*)

in eastern Germany, such as Gustloff and Grossfuss, would have been reactivated.

Moreover, Yugoslavia adopted the MG 42 in the aftermath of the Second World War and put the weapon back into manufacture under the name "1953 model" (MG 42/53 or Sarac). These weapons, very close to the German ones (including their caliber 7.92 mm Mauser), were also sold to anticolonialist movements.

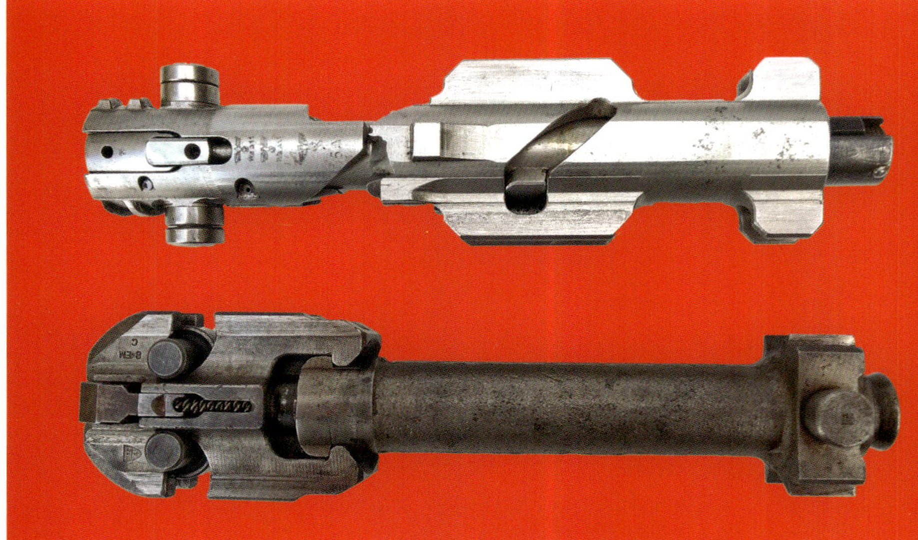

The bolt of the MG 34 (*top*) was of a radically different conception than that of the MG 42 (*bottom*). The removal on the MG 42 of the rotational movement that ensured locking of the MG 34 bolt in the barrel, as well as the movement linked to the release of the firing pin, resulted in a noticeable acceleration of the firing speed of the MG 42.

Comparison of the methods of removing the barrels on the two models. The system is clearly more simple and rapid on the MG 42.

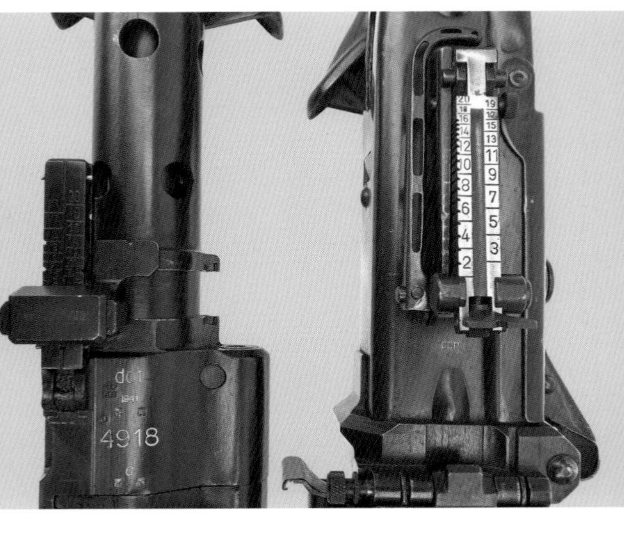

The rear sights of the MG 34 and 42. The antiaircraft finger front sight on the MG 42, folded on the left of the sight, can be seen. This function was provided on the MG 34 by a foldable extension placed on the lower side of the sight.

The top cover bolts on the MG 34 (*left*) and 42 (*right*). Here again, the design of the MG 42 makes handling easier.

FINISH

The first MG 42s were bronzed with the same glossy black (*Duferit*) as other German weapons of the same period. Grinding work was done on the welding zones on the frame to give a cleaner finish.

The bolt, buffer, feed lever, recoil booster, and barrel guide sleeve are a gray-white color due to the surface-hardening treatment they received.

At the end of the war, some parts were phosphate coated. The upper side of the rear sight leaf was polished white to make reading the graduations easier.

The finish worsened during the war, the welding became much more apparent, and the surface of the metal had a more natural appearance. On the weapons made at the end of the war, it is common to see phosphate-coated or even natural-covered parts simply covered with a protective varnish.

Those MG 42s captured by the Soviets on the eastern front were often sandblasted in a rudimentary way before receiving a new bronzing treatment, which gave them a slightly matte finish.

Section of machine gunners with two folded "Lafette" mounts carried by the first and second soldiers in the foreground; the other men carry spare barrel cases and ammunition boxes.

CHAPTER 9

PRODUCTION VARIANTS OF THE MG 42

The MG 42 was manufactured on a large scale soon after its official adoption and until 1945 was subject to only minor modifications.

Bolt handle: Initially, the MG 42s were delivered with a bolt handle with a flat grip. This handle quickly proved to protrude too much, but above all it was difficult to handle. In May 1943, it was replaced by a handle composed of a vertical cylinder connected to a horizontal flat piece in a circular arc and having a locking pawl, and it was much easier to load.*

Foresight base: The early versions had a screw at the rear, reinforcing the fixation of the foresight at the base, while the foresight is simply mounted on a dovetail. In 1943, a simplified version of this part was developed.

Feed tray: This part initially had only a cartridge stop. A guide for the belt links and a cut-and-bent belt hook were added on some makes.

Flash suppressor and recoil booster: The cylindrical flash suppressor with twelve orifices has some variations, as illustrated by our photos.

Another type of very different flash suppressor can be observed on drawings in certain German military manuals, which show it as a "new model" flash suppressor. It seems that this version was never widely used.

The early-production recoil booster had a hole for a 10 mm projectile, then went to 11.5 mm by the end of 1942, and then to 14 mm in 1943 to reduce firing speed.

Bipod: As for the MG 34, the first type of bipod has two slots fitted with a locking system activated by two side buttons. When it is folded under the weapon, the bipod locks on a dowel protruding under the frame.

This arrangement had two flaws:

- The bipod tended to accidentally become unhooked (as on the MG 13 and 34) and would be shunted around under the weapon.
- The blocking of the bipod in the folded position was sometimes difficult to realize if the gunner had to operate it while walking or in darkness.

Two versions of MG 42 flash suppressors. The one on the right is the early model and is now extremely rare (some copies are in existence). *FLP*

This design weakened the resistance of the bipod, and the system locking the bipod in the folded position was easily damaged and was unnecessarily complex to produce.

In October 1943, this system of locking was abandoned and replaced by two simple folded spring-steel loops fixed in one of the oblong holes on the lower side of the frame. The dowel under the frame was removed; its orifice remains under the frame and was sometimes used to fix a ring to attach the transport sling.

* It seems that a number of German gunners were killed while standing up to load and pushing back this first type of bolt handle with the foot.

This officer from the Großdeutschland Division is shooting a preproduction MG 42, recognizable by its seven oblong holes on the side of the cooling jacket. It also has a very rare flash hider with a collar.

Comparison between the frame of an early-production MG 42 (1942) and a late-production one (1945). The finish of the polishing on the welding points is not the same, due to the pressure of productivity. The fixing of the bipods is also completely different.

The two types of sight on the MG 42: flat surface (*on the left*) and centered groove (*on the right*)

A modification notice, issued in February 1944, requested that unit armorers transform the MG 42 fitted with the old holding system of the folded bipod. The bipods were modified by removing the catch and the retaining latches and by adding two spring-steel loops. The locking stud for attachment to the frame was therefore removed.

A new simplification came later with the removal of the height adjustment system on the bipod.

Comparison of the method of fixing on bipods with and without "locking stud"

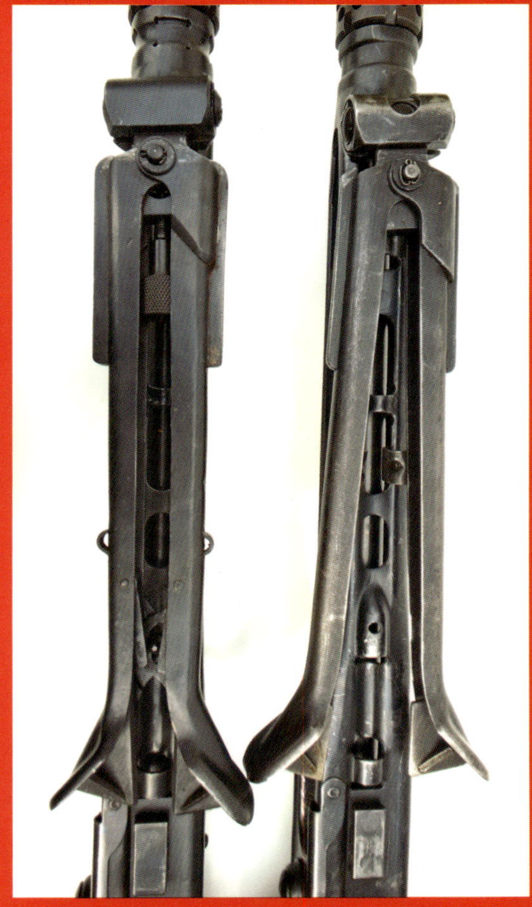

Three versions of an MG 42 bipod

The supply of the MG 42 and the MP 44 assault rifle considerably increased the fire power of the German combat groups when faced with Soviet attack waves, most of them armed with the PPSh 41 submachine gun. *Photo by Marc de Fromont, Royal Army Museum Collection, Brussels*

First version of the MG 42 buttstock in Bakelite (*on the right*). Second version in wood (*on the left*). *In the middle*, a midproduction model modified by the unit armorer by the addition of a metal band along with wood pins at each toe and heel to strengthen it against any impact.

The buttstock of the MG 42 in its last version, with its five loops of wire brazed for reinforcement. This variant was produced from 1944.

1. Buffer with its early single-strand spring. *2.* The buffer with its twisted-wire-manufactured spring.

Grip fixation pin: As on the MG 34, the grip was initially fixed to the frame by two pins, one built into the other; the internal pin was split.

Subsequently, this arrangement was replaced by a single pin, stopped by a split pin (which also had the disadvantage of injuring the shooter's hand).

Recoil spring: Up to the end of 1942, the springs were made in a single strand like those on the MG 34; they were then replaced by more powerful double-strand springs and decreased from a diameter of 25 to 23 mm.

Buttstock: These were made either in Bakelite or wood. Bakelite buttstocks were composed of shavings of fiber that had been soaked in a phenolic resin. They were mounted on weapons from the beginning of production until February 1943. The increasing scarcity of chemical substances required to make Bakelite led to it being abandoned at the end of the war in favor of wood, which was used up to the end of production. Wooden buttstocks, with their tendency to split where they joined the frame, were often reinforced at this point by a metal strip fitted by the unit armorer, starting in the beginning of 1944. From April 1944, buttstocks left the factory systematically reinforced by several rows of metallic wire. The wooden buttstocks also frequently had reinforcing dowels at the two toe and heels.

Comparison of the crimping on the frame. *From left to right*, 42, end of 43 and 44.

(*on right*) Variations of the crimping at the extremity on two frames seen from above

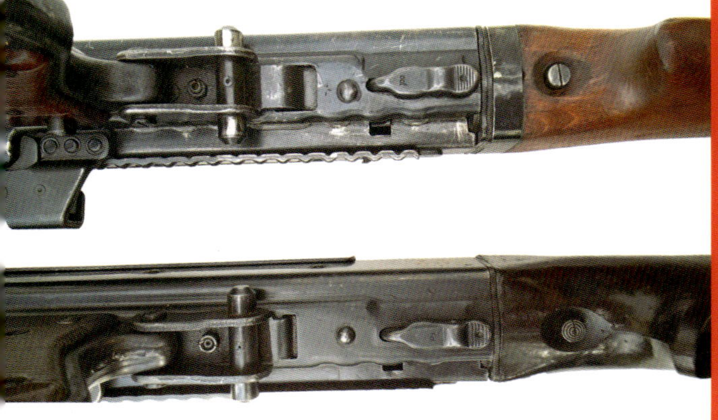

Lower rear side of the frame. *Bottom*: early production; *top*: end of production.

Extremity of the frame: It is possible to observe several types of manufacture of the front part of the frame, where the rectangular profile of this part gave way to a cylindrical profile, just forward of the screw thread on which the flash hider / buffer was fixed. On some weapons, this section of the frame is smooth; on others, there are very thin slits, probably designed to improve the resistance of the metal in this narrower zone.

Band added by a unit armorer to hook the carrying sling

This type of band is visible under the MG 42 in position on a fortified "Tobruk"-type work on a beach in Normandy.

Comparison of cocking handles. *Bottom*: the handle in direct contact with the bolt (the model shown is a copy). It had two drawbacks: the handle was difficult to maneuver and was bulky. The model with a vertical grip corrected both these points.

CONCLUSION: MG 42

As readers may have understood, the production of this weapon was concentrated over a fairly brief period; the manufacture of the MG 42 is therefore relatively homogeneous, despite the possibility of subtle differences, themselves of great interest to collectors.

The variations that have been described here are those identified on the weapons that we have examined and from documents in our possession. There may be other variants.

The MG 42 could without doubt be considered as one of the best illustrations of the new concepts for weapons material that were required during the Second World War. Unlike the MG 34 and other P. 38s designed to withstand sustained use over several decades, the MG 42 (like the MP 40 and later the MP 44) was made for a limited "life." However, in the end these weapons proved to be much tougher than expected, as was demonstrated by the long careers that many of them had after the war.

Foresight on a first-type MG 42. *FLP*

CHAPTER 10

"LAFETTE" MODEL 34 AND 42 MOUNTS

The MG 42 was designed to be fixed on a mount called *die Lafette* in German, which could be fitted with an optical sight if necessary. When set on its mount, the MG 34 was called s.MG (*schweres Maschinengewehr* = heavy machine gun). The MG 42 took up the same mount with several fairly minor adaptations.

The mount and its optics had been developed at the same time as the MG 34. They were an integral part of the technical specifications established by the Reichswehr, which required the future light machine gun to be rapidly transformed into a heavy version, and the mount to be easily converted into a support for antiaircraft fire if necessary.

During the years following its first appearance, this ensemble was considered the most advanced machine gun mount of its time. Its system of projection both for automatic and manual fire, its buffer, and its optics and modular aspect either in land or antiaircraft versions, while at the same time respecting the weight and size restrictions for transport, make it still today a remarkable feat of engineering.

The many possibilities for adjusting the position of angles and the length of the legs meant the mount could be adapted to different types of terrain as well as the type of fire.

The Lafette 34 was specifically dedicated to the MG 34 owing to its method of locking using two half brackets surrounding the barrel, and to the contact interface on the trigger and its two positions of single-shot or continuous-burst fire. Although the Lafette 42 strays from these two points, the relationship between the two mounts is clear. Apart from these two elements, everything that is described in the chapter on the Lafette 34 can also be applied to the model 42.

PRESENTATION OF THE LAFETTE 34

The Lafette 34 was designed in order to be transported on one man's back, since it had a relatively limited weight of 20 kg and was very compact once folded. It had two wide leather straps, allowing it to be carried like a knapsack, with two cleverly positioned pads on the forward leg protecting the carrier's back from the metal.

The mount is made up of three main parts:

Upper frame: This part, made in folded sheet metal, has a frame fixed in a U shape and a rectangular frame, which is the mobile part. The MG is housed in the mobile part by means of two locking points.

The first consists of two claws that enclose the two studs situated behind the grip of the weapon.

The second consisted of a collar that firmly locked the barrel jacket. This collar is designed to be swung on the right to position the barrel jacket in such a way that it can be replaced easily when overheated by firing, without having to separate the weapon from its mount.

Splendid ensemble of a Lafette 42 model known as Gebirgsjäger (mountain troops). The length and side tilt of the rear legs are adjustable, giving it a superior adaptability on rough terrain. The mount here is equipped with an MG.Z 40 optical sight, topped by its indirect-fire collimator. *FLP*

MG 42 mounted on a Lafette mount: a formidable ensemble! The weapon here is equipped with its MG.Z 40 sight and system of lighting. ***Photo by Marc de Fromont, Royal Army Museum Collection, Brussels***

Lafette 42 with a first-type MG 42 and MGZ optics with a periscope

Ecy marking: Fouquet & Franz AG, Rottenburg Neckar.

Fsu marking: Brandenburger Fahrrad und Motorradwerk, Excelsior. The figure 21 indicates the weight of the Lafette.

Detail of the adjustment elements of the Gebirgsjäger Lafette

The mobile frame is held at the front by a buffer containing a powerful compensating spring.

The sliding between the two frames is carried out by four runners held to the fixed frame by four cross-pins, whose heads can appear on the top side of the frame.

The fixed frame has two appendages positioned at its edge: on the right, a bulge encloses a small parallelogram, allowing the angle return of the firing rod to be maintained whatever the position of the mobile frame during recoil or its return to position; on the left, a small rectangular platform with an aluminum dovetail allows an MG.Z 34 sight to be fixed on the mount.

The sight is locked by the tightening of a butterfly screw, which is rendered impossible to lose by its holding pawls pinned on the extremity of its axis. Even though every mount had its designated MG.Z, the Lafette was also commonly used without its optics when the metal gunsights on the MG were sufficient for medium-range fire. This use of the weapon with only the metal gunsights was as common as it was rapid and instinctive.

Support chassis: This part, linking the ensemble to the ground, is made of straight and curved steel tubes welded together and on which three legs are mounted. The two rear legs simply articulate around two left and right pivot points, with the possibility of positioning them under different angles by means of serrated notches. They are locked by means of two wide butterfly screws, which can screw tightly. The front leg is linked to the chassis by a pivot point.

It was deployed with the extension of a cross-link. The length of the leg is adjustable due to the telescopic tube; to extend the front leg simply requires pulling on it while pressing the unlocking handle.

Magazine follower: This element, which is situated at the rear of the mount, is the most complex part (this ensemble was made by a subcontractor of the mount manufacturer). It links the chassis with the support frame of the MG.

The searching-fire unit enables the positioning of the upper mobile unit on site and azimuth. The site orientation (elevation) can be performed manually by the large adjusting knob situated on the left and fitted with adjustable holding pawls, or automatically by an actuator that is activated mechanically by the successive recoils of the MG in its mobile frame during firing. A small bracket, fixed at the left rear under the mobile frame, acts on the actuator under the effect of recoil.

The internals of the searching-fire device are set to elevate the unit with the first five rounds and then depress it with the next four rounds, in a cycle that goes on for the whole burst. The searching-fire device should be set to 0 at all times, except when searching fire is to be deployed.

This remarkable mechanical system enables firing to be started with a preset cone of fire, depending on the configuration of the target.

The orientation azimuth is done manually by sliding the mobile ensemble left to right on a graduated metallic arc fixed to the chassis. This arc is graduated in mils and has two adjustable-thrust stops on notches. Each gradation of the arc is equivalent to a movement of a ten thousandth.

This subgroup also comprises the firing-starter handle on the right. The fixed part of this handle has a small oiler, closed by a stopper, on which a

Code "axx," indicating manufacture by Linden & Funke kg, Iserloh

Code "cqi," assigned to the manufacturer Heinrich H. Klüssendorf Werkzeuge, Berlin-Spandau

MG 34 in antiaircraft firing position, with its AA extension unit mounted on the Lafette

Lafette ready for land fire with the legs in position

Utilization of the Lafette in position for antiaircraft fire

Firing controls of an end-of-production Lafette. The fixed grip no longer has its oil buret, and the mobile handle is no longer in pressed metal but is made from one piece of wood.

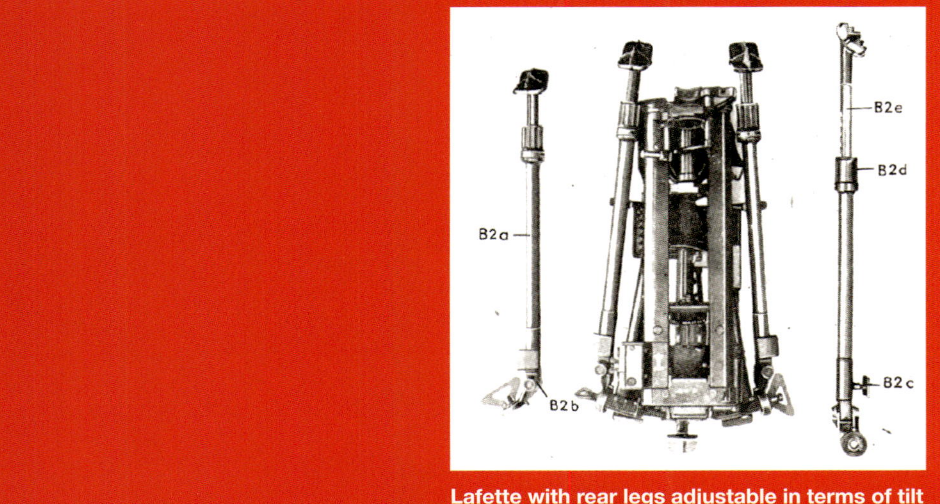

Lafette with rear legs adjustable in terms of tilt and length

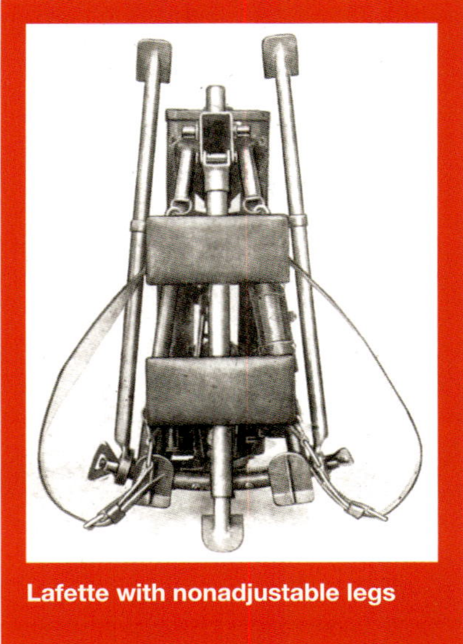
Lafette with nonadjustable legs

brush is fixed. This ingenious element means that this precise and complex mechanism can be maintained regularly.

The principal function of the Lafette 34 was to fire at land targets, but the aluminum tubular extension housed in the cylindrical protuberance extending beyond the front of the mount meant it was also designed for antiaircraft fire. The upper end of the AA (antiaircraft) extension was fitted with a top forked piece with a semicircular bracket, allowing the MG to be set up by means of a central circular rail situated on the cooling jacket (under the rear sight).

This option was often used by the gunners, since it meant they did not have to transport the tripod, specifically designed for antiaircraft fire, with the Lafette 34.

This last function of the mount demonstrates clearly the accomplished versatility of its design.

On both sides of the vertical tubular extension for antiaircraft fire, there were two small, horizontal pivot pins to attach the Lafette to the external supports of the carts conveying the MG 34 for antiaircraft fire (MG-Zwilling-Sockel 36). This twin mount had been designed so both machine guns could be quickly removed and it could immediately be used as an infantry weapon if necessary, mounted on their Lafette 34.

During transport, both Lafette mounts, protected by their respective covers, were fixed on the rear outside board in order to keep the inside of the cart as free as possible.

MG 34 in action on a Lafette equipped with an MGZ. The group is protected by the building so as to be less visible to the enemy. *NARA*

DEVELOPMENTS AND VARIANTS OF THE LAFETTE 34

The main principle of this mount barely evolved from its putting into service in 1936 until the end of the war.

Indirect-fire tables in aluminum were not planned on the first versions. They first appeared in September 1937, and the unit armorers had the task of adding them to the mounts already in service. They were fixed by four rivets on the rear side of the fire elevator.

The spare bolt box and spent-case-deflector plate were also absent on the first mounts to be delivered.

These accessories were not put into production until 1940. The mounts that did not have them originally were, for the most part, fitted with them later in the field.

The legs on most of the mounts had slightly curved bases for an improved grip on the ground. A variant from the beginning of production had bases with triangular-shaped tips; it is likely that this design was to enable the mounts to adhere to hard or slippery surfaces such as frozen terrain or ice.

Rest pads, covered in leather when they left the factory, were damaged due to handling and impacts in the field. Renovations carried out in the units were made using canvas or camouflaged canvas.

An MG mounted on a Lafette and transported on a wooden sledge, turned against its former owners by Soviet partisans. ***DR***

The only significant variant of the Lafette model 34 is its mount with extendable legs. This recognizable and rare variant had telescopic legs at the rear. It was designed for mountain troops (*Gebirgslafette*).

Two versions were developed for this use:

- the first, with wing nuts to modify the position of the rear legs
- a second, later model had a springed push button

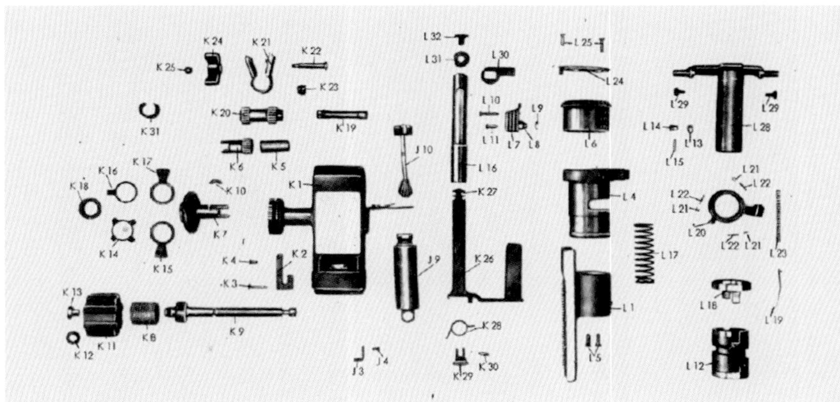

Parts making up the adjusting mechanism of the Lafette

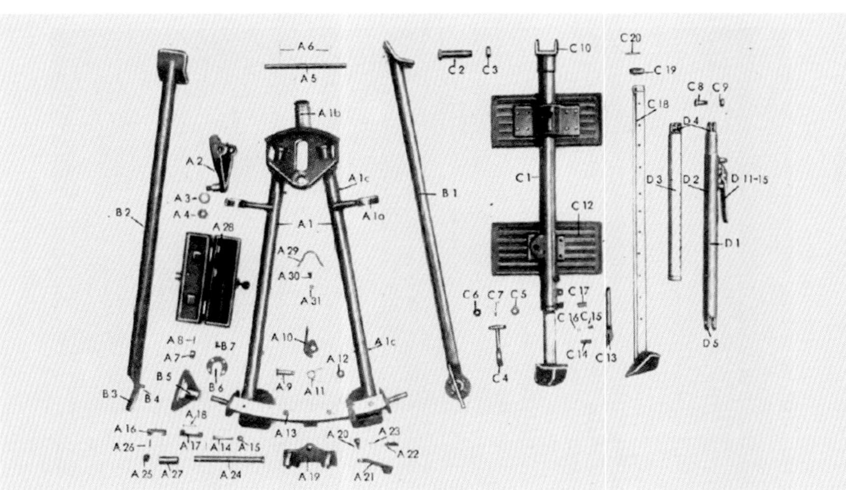

The many parts of the tripod. The Lafette 34 is made up of two hundred parts. Its disassembly is therefore not within everyone's reach!

MG 42 in an entrenchment near Berlin in 1945. The Lafette is a version with adjustable rear legs. The antiaircraft extension can be seen on the left side, along with a case for the spare barrel.

On both versions the rear legs were extended by unscrewing the large rings around the telescopic tubes and then tightening them once the desired length was reached.

MARKINGS AND PROOF STAMPS

Various markings, codes, and references are found in different places on the model 34 mount. They are used to identify the mount or to use it in the different configurations.

The most-obvious markings are situated on the steel part at the rear of the upper frame: the manufacturer's code, a serial number followed by a letter, the year of manufacture in full or in code form, and one or two Waffenamt (WaA) inspection stamps.

The serial number is also found on the rear arc. On those mounts from the beginning of production, the WaA stamps were on numerous parts such as pins and runners, the rear arc and its push buttons, the trigger plunger, the MG cradle, the aluminum base, the sights, and the head of the actuator. The manufacturer's codes can also be found on the front of the chassis and the forward leg.

The stamps are less numerous on the end-of-war mounts due to the simplification of the inspection procedures.

It is estimated that between 100,000 and 150,000 Lafette mounts (both 34 and 42 models) were produced during the war. This relatively small number of mounts compared to the great number of MGs made is explained by the fact that many MG 34s were used only on a bipod in the light-machine-gun version (Leichtes Maschinengewehr). In addition, the MG 34 was used on other types of mounts (antiaircraft tripods, twin mounts, various fortress or vehicle mounts), which will be reviewed later.

SEARCHING-FIRE UNIT

This part was made as a complete subunit, by several subcontractors, for the assemblers of the mounts. The stamps on the left side of the magazine follower are specific and independent from those of the manufacturers of the mounts. These markings indicated the manufacturer's code, the year of manufacture, and its serial number. The serial number is completely independent from that on the Lafette chassis, and therefore no link should be sought between the two units.

PAINTED MARKINGS ON MODEL 34 MOUNTS

In addition to the stamps struck on the metal, references in paint can also be found in various positions to facilitate the operation and use of the mount by the gunners.

On the rear leg-swiveling balls, the cast index could be underlined in red or white to make them more visible. The front leg and the transversal link have locking holes surrounded in white paint to facilitate adjustments in predefined positions or on the orders of the unit commander.

The mechanisms of the automatic actuator or the manual adjusting also had their index and figures underlined in white.

The majority of mounts also had numbers painted on the upper frame near the base of the optics or at the rear of the frame. This number is that of the MG.Z 34 paired with this mount. On certain mounts this number is found struck on a small plate riveted on the sheet metal at the rear. Unit numbers painted on the upper frame of the mount and even the indication of its weight can also be found.

Rapid change of position: the weapon and its mount are transported by three men. The setup could therefore be carried out swiftly.

PAINTING ON THE MOUNTS

The shades of the paint applied in the factory were standardized and were developed over time. The paint applied in the factory was mixed with an additive containing a hardening agent, and everything was heated in order to improve shock resistance. The parts were painted before assembly, but some parts were treated by black bronzing (nuts and bolts), or a green or yellow protective coating for the parts in aluminum (preset of the actuator, buffer, and optics base).

The elements designed to slide or that were subject to friction were not painted. The AA extension mount and its two pivot pins at the front, for example, remained in their raw state, which was justified by the fact that the friction caused by the assembly would have caused the paint to wear. The extension tubes of the front leg and its transversal brace were not painted for the same reason.

The upper part of the magazine follower as well as its mobile racks were not painted. The arc and its bolts and screws were not painted.

The forward leg rest pads were mounted and sewn on two rectangular metallic frames perforated on the edge, which were fixed on the front leg once they were painted.

Transport, bad weather, friction, and impacts from equipment, weapons, and ammunition belts tested the mounts severely, and the units maintained them with the means at their disposal.

In this context, they were most often repainted with a brush, using the original shade in force at the time of restoration. Depending on the conditions and theaters of operation, camouflage tints were sometimes applied: white in snowy areas, sandy yellow for desert areas, etc.

Lafette Manufacturers' Identification Codes

		Manufacturer's Name	Code	Year of Production
Lafette 34	Frame	Excelsior, Brandenburger Fahrrad und Motorradwerk	S323/fsu	1936–42
		Metallindustrie Schönebeck AG	S652/dar	1938–42
		Siemens Elektrowärmer G.m.b.H., Werk Sörnewitz	Switz	1939
		Hülsbeck & Fürst, Schlossfabrik	S968 / btm / SXO	1940–41
		Fouquet & Franz AG, Rottenburg Neckar	ecy	1942–43
		Rudolf Schluckebier & Co., Eisenbahnbedarf	eat	1943–44
	Elevator	Heinrich H. Klüssendorf Werkzeuge, Berlin-Spandau	"HHK"/30/cql/RE	
		Linden & Funke kg, Iserlohn	736/axx/YV	
		Brunsviga-Maschinenwerke, Grimme, Natalis & Co. AG	GNC/ckk	
		Präzisionswerke Brüninghaus & Co.	bga/TM	
		Hermann Werbig Waggonfabrik, Nossen	bkh	

		Manufacturer's Name	Code	Year of Production
Lafette 42	Frame	Excelsior, Brandenburger Fahrrad und Motorradwerk	fsu	1942–44
		Metallindustrie Schönebeck AG	dar	1943–44
		Hülsbeck & Fürst, Schlossfabrik	btm / SXO	1943–45
	Elevator	Heinrich H. Klüssendorf Werkzeuge, Berlin-Spandau	Cql/RE	
		Linden & Funke kg, Iserlohn	axx/YV	
		Präzisionswerke Brüninghaus & Co.	bga/TM	
		Metallindustrie Schönebeck AG	dar	

CHAPTER 11

MG.Z 34 AND MG.Z 40 MOUNTED OPTICAL SIGHTS AND THEIR ACCESSORIES

Manufacturer's marking: "ddx" for Voigtländer Braunschweig

Manufacturer's marking: "cxn" for Busch Rathenow

Manufacturer's marking: Wichmann

The MG. Zieleinrichtung 34 (abbreviated to MG.Z 34), when associated with the Lafette 34 mount, meant that long-distance direct or indirect fire could be carried out. The word *Zieleinrichtung* can be loosely translated as "target acquisition system."

This optical sight first appeared in 1936, but it was not immediately available in sufficient quantities to equip the units. It was first supplied to units in 1937. Initially, machine gunners of the new Wehrmacht had to carry on mounting old ZF 12s on their Lafette 34, destined for the MG 08 machine gun. The ZF 12 had the advantage of being available in large quantities at that time but was designed only for direct fire. For indirect fire, a special sight, complementary to the ZF 12, had to be used: the MG Richtaufsatz (M.G.R.A.). As for the presentation of the Lafette, all descriptions concerning the MG.Z 34 apply also to the MG.Z 40.

PRESENTATION

The MG.Z 34 is an optical sight for direct and indirect fire. It has a magnification of 3 and a field of vision of 13° at 1,000 meters. Its base has two spirit levels, so the mount can be positioned in a perfectly horizontal position on both axes, before any firing setup is carried out. To prepare for indirect fire, the MG.Z 34 can pivot on 360° to carry out angle measurements. This is done by aiming for the red base of the RK 31 theodolite tripod used by fire observers that have a clear view on the grouping of the MG and on the target.

Fallschirmjäger* in position behind his MG 42 on a Lafette. The MG.Z 40 is fitted with its indirect-fire collimator. Note that the cover of the ammunition box is used as a feeding ramp for the cartridge belt. *BA

Collection of different optical elements of the MG 34 and 42.
From left to right:

- **ZF 12 and the MGRA gunsights, descended from the MG 08 equipment of the First World War; these optical sights were used for training MG 34 gunners in 1937–38.**
- **MG.Z 34 with its periscope**
- **MG.Z 40**

MG.Z 34 bearing the code "ddx": Voigtländer Braunschweig

From left to right: Azimuth and elevating knobs of the MG.Z 34 and the first version of MG.Z 40. *On the left*, a second type of MG.Z 40 that no longer has the indirect-fire operation. The indirect-fire band has been replaced by sheet metal with a protective gold-colored coating.

The elevation adjustment system of the MG.Z 34 had two modes:

- The first was for direct fire. The firer adjusted the firing distance by turning the elevation knob while bringing the index (situated under the small window) on the graduation of the desired distance. The distance was then directly indicated in meters. This was the method of use when the firer had a clear view of the target.

- The second mode was for indirect fire. For this configuration, the firer turned the flap 180° to cover the direct-fire adjustment window. The indication "indirekt" would then appear on the knob. The elevation of the sight then had to be set in relation to the indications from the fire observers, which indicated a setting in angle in mils. The gunner then adjusted his sight by turning the knob until the index (situated on the right side) reached the desired graduation.

This graduation in mils is situated in an arc positioned vertically to the right of the sight. In a horizontal position, the index is in front of the 300-mils graduation, which corresponds to an elevation of 0 degrees. This method of firing was for when the target was not directly visible by the shooter (target too far away, or behind an obstacle or firing over friendly troops).

Seven manufacturers produced he MG.Z 34, and ten produced the MG.Z 40. The name of the maker is indicated in plain text on the early-production sights. It was then identified by means of a three-letter code.

The MG.Z 34 was made from 1936 to the beginning of 1943. Manufacturers then directed their means of production on the new MG.Z 40, which appeared at the end of 1942 and was therefore used more with the Lafette 42, destined for the MG 42.

COLORS AND MARKINGS OF THE MG.Z

Manufacturers painted the MG.Z 34 in different shades of light gray and green, and, for the MG.Z 40, gray and sand yellow.

The manufacturer's markings were underlined in white paint. All the MG.Zs had a serial number; the markings (serial number, manufacturer) that made up the identity of the optics were stamped on the front side.

Indirect-fire collimator mounted on the telescope of a first-version MG.Z 40

MG.Z 34 and MG.Z 40 optical sights in their transport boxes, with all the accessories

MG.Z 40 and its box. The MG.Z 34 boxes were not identified by a marking on the cover. *MRA*

Marking of the manufacturer (f) lww: Huet & Co.: Flammarion binoculars, a well-known French optical firm, whose services were requisitioned by the occupier.

MG.Z Manufacturers				
Manufacturer	**End of production codes**		**Optics manufactured, MG.Z 34**	**Optics manufactured, MG.Z 40**
Busch Rathenow	cxn		X	X
Voigtländer Braunschweig	ddx		X	X
G. Heyde Dresden	bwt		X	X
Hildebrand Wichmann Werke, Freiberg & Berlin	cmd or cme		X	X
J.-D. Moeller Wedel	dhq		X	X
Franz Kuhlmann Wilhelmshaven	bvu		X	X
Hensoldt & Söhen, Wetzlar	bmj		X	
Ungarische Optiche Werke	gug			X
Zeiss Ikon	dpw			X
French manufacture under German control	During the war	Postwar for the French army		
Huet & Co. binoculars Flammarion (f)	lww	L.785		X
Optique et Mécanique de Haute précision (f)	lwy	L.786		X

The optics were often identified by the units, who painted the number of the corresponding MG on the top of the circular cover with a brush. This allowed the rapid pairing of the right optics and the right mount with the weapon.

The round, cross-shaped, or triangular symbols, marked in blue near the name of the manufacturer, indicate the types of grease used for the internal workings:

- inscription "KF" = the grease used until 1940, the Invarol type, for use with temperatures to −20°C
- a blue circle = the Vakuumfett 1416 type of grease, used for temperatures for temperatures to −40°C
- a blue cross = Instrumentfett 1442 grease for temperatures to −40°C
- a blue triangle = grease used for a range of temperatures from −40°C up to +50°C

ACCESSORIES

The MG.Z was delivered in a metallic transport box, with wooden, felt-covered spacers and spaces for the lenses and the cleaning brush inside.

The boxes destined for the MG.Z were painted in dark green (*Olivgrün*) and marked with black or white paint on the inside of the cover. The numbers of the MG or the units were also often painted on the outside or inside of the cover.

Firing position of an early MG 34 (jacket with four holes); the shooter has removed the butt. One of the observers is using an EM34 rangefinder to measure the distance to a target.

The "cme" manufacturer's marking: Hildebrand Wichmann Werke, Freiberg & Berlin

The "dhq" manufacturer's marking: J.-D. Moeller Wedel

Collection of material necessary to define the parameters (site, azimuth, distance), indispensable for carrying out indirect fire:

- rangefinder Entfernungsmesser 34 (EM34) with its tripod
- theodolite Richtkreis 31 (RK31) (due to its size the tripod is not seen here) with its periscope
- inclinometer Deckungswinkelmesser
- measuring triangle Messdreieck 34
- firing tables (the cover of the book shown here has been treated against dampness with a varnish)
- pair of binoculars
- compass
- map holder with maps of the site and measurement grids

Stakes for indirect fire with transport case for the belt. This accessory was also used for orienting mortar fire.

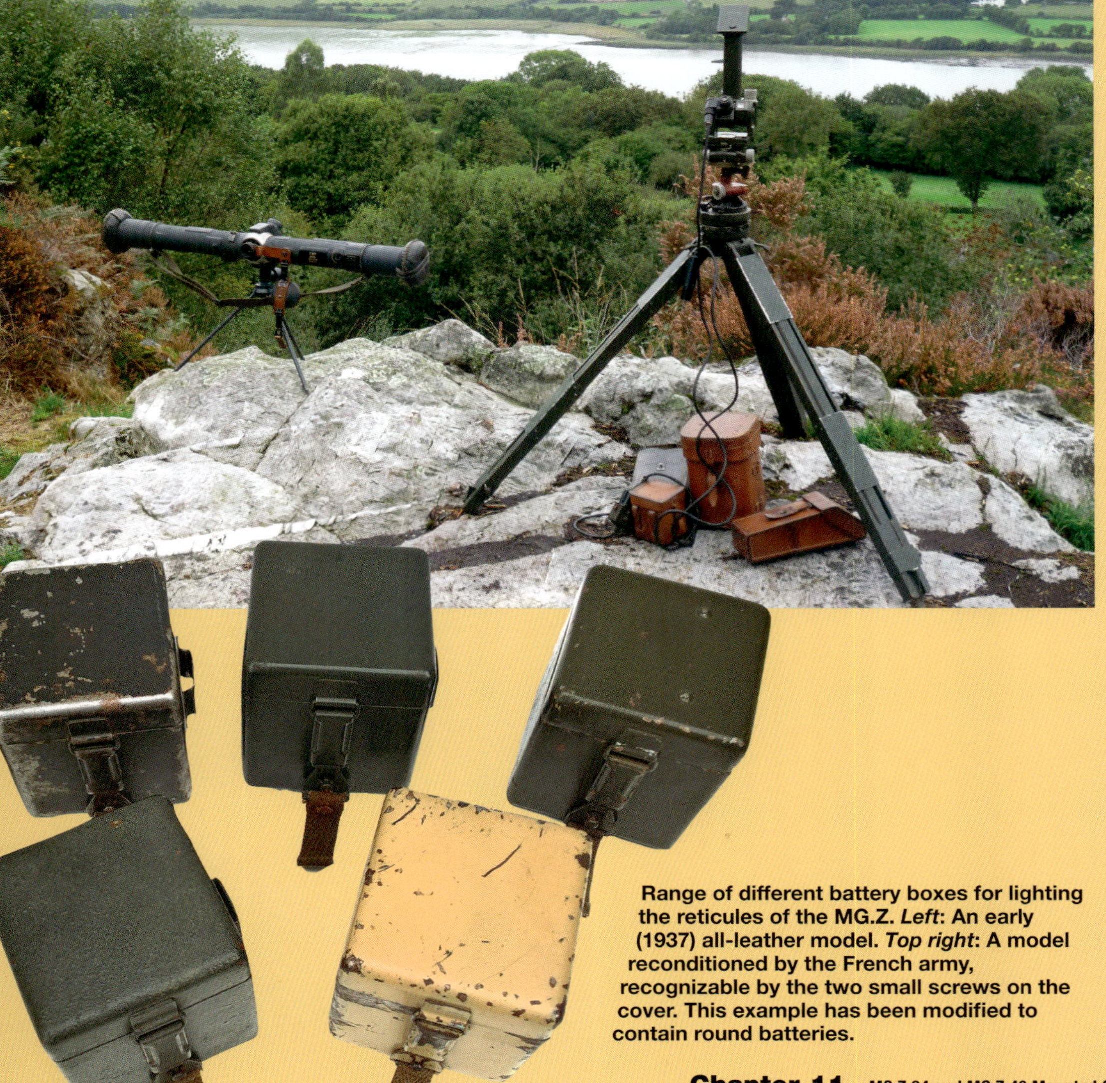

An EM34 rangefinder and an RK31 theodolite in a high position

Range of different battery boxes for lighting the reticules of the MG.Z. *Left*: An early (1937) all-leather model. *Top right*: A model reconditioned by the French army, recognizable by the two small screws on the cover. This example has been modified to contain round batteries.

This battery box was designed to contain three 1.5V, flat-shaped batteries. Only the one placed facedown was in service, the other two being kept as spare.

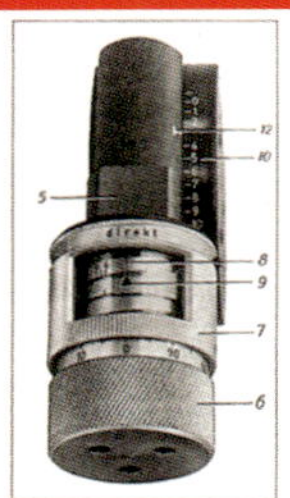

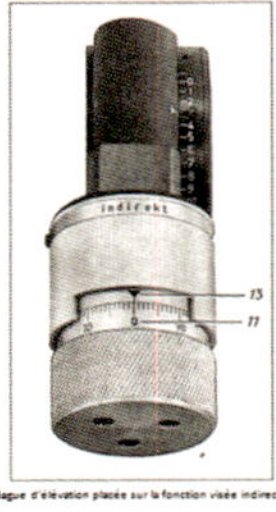

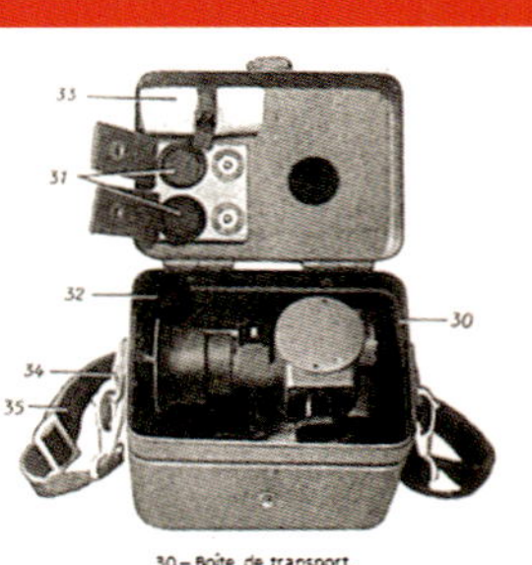

Description of the MG.Z and its accessories

MG crew preparing its mount and positioning the MG.Z

In addition to the MG.Z, the box also contained two small solar filters, a brush, and a square of fabric for cleaning, as well as a small collimator, detachable for the MG.Z 40. A periscope appeared in 1942 and could also be housed in the box. This periscope was designed to allow the firer to keep his head slightly lower and therefore less exposed to enemy fire (particularly from snipers). A specific canvas strap, with two highly distinctive hooks, meant it could be carried over the shoulder.

A lot of German optics were designed to be lit from the inside so that the reticule was visible in dull light. To this effect, the MG.Z had a small window with a dovetail above the eyepiece. This window allows a bulb to be fitted. The lighting system was fitted with a small flap, controlling the amount of light that could be adjusted by the operator if necessary.

The bulb was powered, via plugs and a cord, by a box containing flat-shaped batteries. The box could house three batteries so that there were always two spare. The battery in use was facedown, whereas the two others were placed faceup. This box, made in leather up to 1938, was subsequently made in sheet metal to be more economical with resources and for a quicker manufacture.

The firer also had a small light stick, which allowed him to see the settings that had to be made in the half light. The two cables were linked to the plug from the battery box via a double connector with a switch that cut the lighting only for the cable going to the MG.Z 34.

Periscope mounted on the optical sight of an MG.Z. The eye cup has been replaced on the periscope.

This photo showing an MG 42 with a Volksturm rifle and a Panzerfaust 60 evokes the last combat of the Volksturm, with the Allies arriving in Germany 1945. The ease of manufacture of the MG 42, which required only a minimum of machining, allowed German industry to continue to maintain large-scale supplies despite the destruction from Allied strategic bombing. *Photo by Marc de Fromont, Royal Army Museum Collection, Brussels*

CHAPTER 12

MOUNTS FOR ANTIAIRCRAFT FIRE

Apart from the "Lafette," the Wehrmacht used a great number of mounts for the MG throughout the Second World War. Some mounts were made quickly, depending on the context and the desired use. Since an exhaustive inventory of the material used is virtually impossible, only the most-common models will be presented here.

INFANTRY MOUNTS

The extension for Lafette (Lafettenaufsatzstück): This unit consists of a cradle (*Aufsatzstück*) supporting the weapon, mounted at the top of an aluminum tubular support (*Stütze*), adaptable on the Lafette. This system, put into service starting in 1936 with one supplied per MG, enabled the weapon to be raised to carry out antiaircraft fire on planes flying at low altitude. Steel tubes were also made at the end of the war.

The 34 model tripod (Dreibein 34): This is a solid tripod with extendable legs, based on the one that existed for the MG 08/15. It is mounted on the MG by means of the same support (*Aufsatzstück*) as described above. To facilitate its transport by land troops, this tripod was made in aluminum. At the end of the war, these tripods started to be made from steel, for economic reasons.

MG Sockel 41 and 42: Less widely used than the previous two, this mount is made up of a sort of tripod stool extended by a long vertical arm supporting the machine gun. This support takes up a principle initiated by the Czech manufacturer Brno for the ZB 26 light machine gun and naturally taken up by its British descendant: the Bren. The long arm of the base of the model 41 machine gun ends with a single half bracket to fix the MG 34. On the model 42, this part ends with a support cradle with a buffer.

MG 34 in antiaircraft position on a Dreibein 34 tripod. Two full ammunition boxes are used to stabilize the mount during firing.

Very fine example of an antiaircraft mount on a rotating-leg Fliegerdrehstütze 36, with an MG 42 in A-A position (firing sight and *Trommel* engaged). This mount was fixed on the floor of light vehicles and had very good stability and was less bulky. It had a gear crank to control the elevation. In rest position, the MG was blocked vertically, with its handle locked in a housing. *MRA*

***Top*: The Dreibein 34, with aluminum legs, here equipped with a support (*Lager*) for use with an MG 34. *Bottom*: A Dreibein 40, smaller than its predecessor and entirely in steel; the head is fitted with a lager for MG 42s. The locking tab of the MG has been modified by the addition of a small sphere, making handling easier.**

Tobrouk type of fortress mount. *D Horm Jersey*

Mount for hand cart: The Wehrmacht used small hand carts (Handkarren If 8), for infantrymen to transport heavy loads (in particular, ammunition boxes). These carts could also be towed behind a motorcycle or a Kettenkrad-type motorcycle half-track. The technical review, distributed in the units for the use of master armorers in April 1942, published the plan of a rudimentary machine gun support that could be made in unit and mounted on hand carts so the MG 34 could be set up on the indispensable *Aufsatzstück*.

The model 15 antiaircraft claw mount (Fliegerabwebrpivot 15): This name designates a small mount designed to be fixed to the top of a tree trunk, cut to the height of a man, by means of three claws that were also used for MG 13 and MG 15 machine guns, often used by the Luftwaffe for the defense of aerodromes.

Magnificent overhead view of a Zwillingsokel 36, assigned for the antiaircraft protection from a train

Twinned-mount 1936 model (Zwillingsockel 36): At the beginning of the war in the German infantry, this type of mount was set up on a model 36 horse-drawn cart (MG-Wagen 36) towed by a team of two or four horses and accompanied the infantry columns on foot. For many French people, this image has become inseparable from the invasion of France by the Wehrmacht in 1940.

MG 34, with the mounts on a circular rail on a Tobrouk-type small bunker

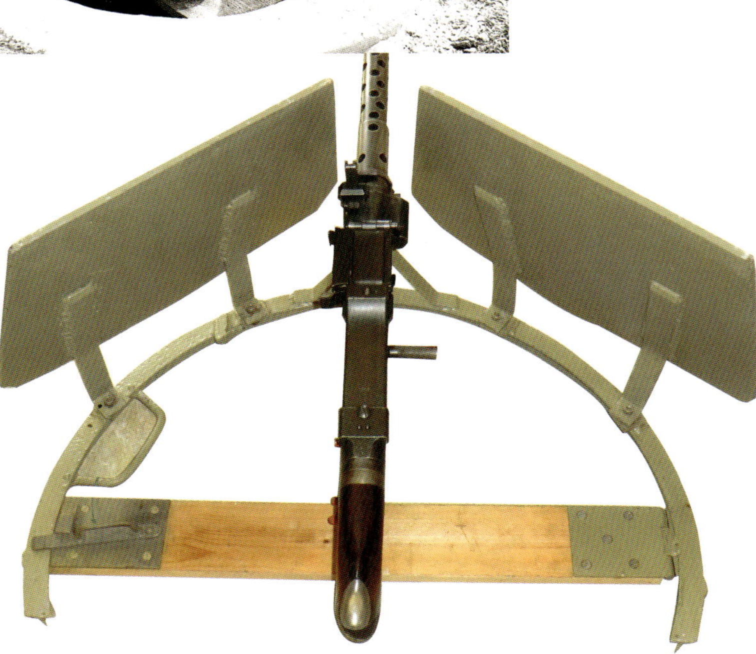

Tobrouk mount with ball mask. *D Horm Jersey*

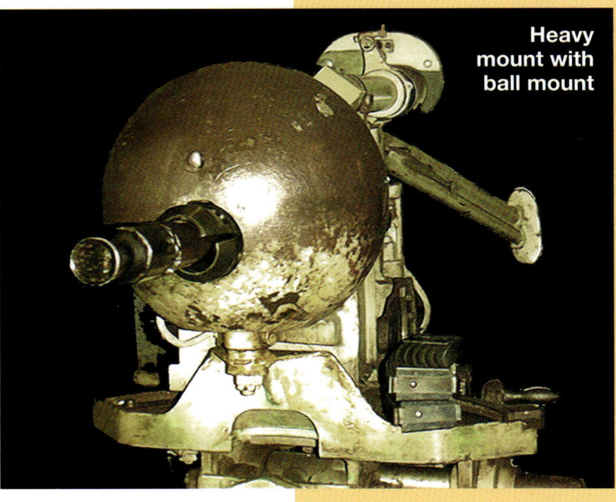

Heavy mount with ball mount

Early MG 34 (four holes) mounted on an Sd.Kfz.221 reconnaissance vehicle. The MG is fed by a double-drum Patronentrommel 34, on which the number of the MG has been transferred by paint.

Twinning was formed of two MG 34 or 42 machine guns with arming from the right side of the receiver and feeding from the left by two specific belt boxes: "Patronenkasten 36," each containing 150 cartridges per belt.

The decision to use standard machine guns on this double mount was dictated by the desire to conserve the possibility of using them separate from the cart, like ordinary infantry machine guns. To this end, two Lafette model 34 mounts were transported at the rear of the model 36 cart. These mounts were then bolted by two small pivot pins on both sides of the AA extension tube connection. During transport on the cart, both mounts were protected by canvas covers.

The buttstocks and bipods, unnecessary in this configuration, were generally disassembled when the machine guns were set up on the twin mount. A trigger connector permitted the triggers on both weapons to be used simultaneously. An antiaircraft ring sight was positioned between the two elements. The shooter oriented the mount manually and with the legs for the orientation and azimuth. Even though it was ineffective against modern airplanes flying at high altitude that appeared during the war, the twin-mount 1936 model continued to be used on very diverse supports: auxiliary ships of the Kriegsmarine, rail convoys, fortified locations, etc.

MOUNTS FOR WHEELED OR HALF-TRACK VEHICLES

Mounts for Fliegerdrehstütze 36 nonarmored vehicles: Put into service from 1940 onward, this A-A fire support was made up of two telescopic tubes with a gear crank for adjusting the height. This tube was designed to be fixed on the flatbed of a vehicle. The tube supported the weapon by means of a forked piece (*Aufsatzstück*), also used on various other mounts.

An arc welded on the body of the tube served as a rest position for the grip of the machine gun and meant that the weapon could be maintained in an almost vertical position during transport. This mount was commonly used at the beginning of the war for the defense of nonarmored vehicles. It had the advantage of offering good firing stability, considering its relatively small footprint.

MG 42 set up on an Fliegerdrehstütze 36 mount fixed at the rear of a Jagdtiger abandoned in a German village in 1945. Note that the MG has been easily neutralized by removing the flash hider and its booster cone.

Montage detail

Various light assemblies: Wehrmacht reconnaissance groups widely used motorcycles fitted with a sidecar and generally armed with a machine gun. These sidecars have become symbolic of the German forces of the Second World War, and there is scarcely a film dedicated to this period without a scene with one of these vehicles. The presence of a driving wheel on the side gave it astonishing all-terrain and handling ability.

This association of motorcycle / machine gun conferred an increased mobility to the machine gun, and it could be rapidly positioned. The presence of an MG 34 mounted at the front of a sidecar on a forked piece sliding on a horizontal bar also meant that the sidecar was able to cover its retreat, if necessary, with a few machine gun bursts of fire.

It is with this in mind that some all-terrain light vehicles of the *Kubelwagen* type (German equivalent to the American jeep) were fitted with this machine gun support.

Mounts for infantry support vehicles: From the middle of the war, the half-track vehicles of the Sd.Kfz. series (*Sonderkraftfahrzeug*: special vehicle) were equipped with two machine guns, MG 34 and then MG 42: one, generally mounted at the front of the hull of the vehicle, was protected by a shaped shield and was used to ensure fire support for the grenadiers arriving in half-track vehicles. The other, generally positioned at the rear of the hull, was used more for defense against aircraft.

MG 34 on a mount specific to Sd.Kfz. half-track vehicles. The optical sight is a ZF 12 fitted with a periscope, based on the model of the RK31, which keeps the firer sheltered from direct fire.

MOUNTS FOR ARMORED VEHICLES

Internal mounts and turret mounts: The first armored vehicles, developed in the greatest secrecy by the Reichswehr, were armed with MG 13 machine guns. The shape of the barrel jacket of the MG 34 was deliberately copied from the MG 13 so that the MG 34 jacket could be replaced by the MG 13 jacket, without having to carry out modifications to the turret mount.

The MG 34 was the principal turret weapon of German armored vehicles only at the beginning of the war. Later, machine guns were associated with barrels that continued to increase (20, 37, 75, 88 mm, etc.), then were relegated to the role of vehicle defense weapons such as an antipersonnel hull machine gun or a machine gun positioned at the exterior of the turret, with the main function of AA fire.

Hull mounts. Throughout the war, the MG 34 remained the principal defense weapon for armored vehicles. In this role, it was mounted on a ball mask placed in the hull of the vehicle, and was used by the radio operator, who could use it against enemy infantry.

The initial model of the hull mount with a square window, called Kugelblende 30, was replaced by the Kugelblende 60, with a round window, in the middle of the war.

Bipod of an MG 34 equipped with two metallic parts so the MG can slide on the circular rail of a Tobrouk.

In May 1940, General Heinz Guderian during the French campaign in France onboard his command Sd.Kfz., armed with an MG 34 on a rotating mount. *BA*

Schartenlafette 08 mount. This mount is a hybrid between an MG 08 and the Lafette of the MG 34. It was designed to be used in bunkers and could slide on a rail to achieve its firing position after opening the armored firing flap in the bunker.

Since these ball masks were not adapted to the shape of the square-section part of the MG 42 barrel, when the Wehrmacht abandoned the MG 34 in favor of the MG 42 as an infantry machine gun, it continued production of the MG 34 at the Brno factory in occupied Czechoslovakia, with the sole objective of continuing to equip its panzers.

External mounts. During the Polish, Belgian, and French campaigns, the Wehrmacht, to whom the Luftwaffe guaranteed the mastery of the air, was not really concerned about equipping its panzers with A-A machine guns.

At that period, the armor was doubtless judged to be sufficient for an isolated panzer to resist the bullets from a light machine gun fired from a marauding aircraft. Indeed, at that time, the Allies did not have aircraft specialized in the attack of armored vehicles (or at least not to any great extent). As for large concentrations of armored vehicles, they were generally protected by powerful detachments of antiaircraft artillery.

From 1941 onward, the model 41 turret mount (Fliegerbeschussgerät 41) entered into service. Mounted on a circular rail surrounding the cupola of the tank commander (*Kommandantenkuppel*), which meant that the machine gun could be turned rapidly in the direction of an attack, this antiaircraft mount had been developed by the Daimler-Benz AG firm in their Berlin-Marienfelde factory.

The following year, an improved version appeared that was christened Fliegerbeschussgerät 42. This mount was used for the MG 34 and then the MG 42 machine guns, which were used on a large scale for antiaircraft defense toward the end of the war. However, even with its rate of fire of 1,200 shots per minute, an MG 42 provided only an illusory protection against swift, modern aircraft, which were both well protected and heavily armed (20 to 40 mm guns, rockets, etc.) used by the Allies to destroy armored vehicles.

FORTRESS MOUNTS

Countless models of fortress mounts were used in the thousands of bunkers that were scattered throughout occupied Europe by the Todt organization over four years.

The most spectacular fortress mount is certainly the ball mask equipped with an MG 34 and fitted with an optical sight. This type of unit was destined for arming covered pillboxes.

The illustrations in this article show various mounts designed to be set up in the embrasures of fortified works.

The small round bunkers, nicknamed Tobrouk, were made to receive an MG 34 or 42 on its Lafette or mounted on various other locally made mounts.

Schartenlafette 08 Fortress mount on a bunker in Norway. *BA*

CHAPTER 13

ACCESSORIES

The multiple accessories supplied for the MG 34 and 42 responded to the desire to make these weapons multipurpose machine guns, able to be used by the infantry, on light and heavy vehicles, and at sea.

This universal scope required that the boxes, magazines, and tools could maintain the weapon at full capacity and in any situation whether it was at −50°C in the Russian snow or the heat of +50°C in the sands of Cyrenaica. We will discuss the tools here and will comment on the photos of the other accessories.

MG GUNNER'S TOOL POUCH (*WERKZEUGTASCHE*)

This pouch, worn at the belt, was the basic accessory for every MG 34 gunner. The first pouches were common to the MG 34 and 13. These early models had a strap worn across the shoulder but did not have belt loops. The later versions had belt loops when the strap was removed from use.

Some early versions had a housing under the cover with metal clips, where a barrel caliber gauge was kept in a small Bakelite container. From 1942 onward, there was a variant of the pouch with the internal compartment in sheet metal modified to house the MG 42 A-A firing sight, the leg of which was longer than on the MG 34.

The MG 42 sight had to be positioned at an angle in the pouch. It would appear that there was never a specific pouch created for the GL 42, but that the MG 34 pouches were simply adapted by cutting the AA firing-sight compartment. Even though the pouch remained the same from the outside, some elements specific to the MG 42 were replaced (spare bolt, A-A firing sight, shell extractor, flash-hider clamping key).

The *Werkzeugtasche* has the accessories indispensable for the operation of a weapon and for the execution of repairs in the field. Throughout the war, the following elements were found:

- An asbestos-lined canvas hand protector. This accessory could be placed on the outside of the pouch, under its closing strap, so the user could grasp it quickly in order to change the burning-hot barrel without having to open the pouch.
- a complete spare bolt
- an A-A firing sight (*Kreishorn*)
- a broken shell extractor (*Hülsenreissern* or *Hülsenentferner*), of which there are several variations

Various parts for the MG 34 contained in a Waffenmeister spare box. These parts come from the box marked "E," for *Erganzüngkasten* (additional box). Three cylindrical containers were destined for immersing the elements of the flash hider.

Spare parts for the MG 42. There are parts for the bolts, a bolt head extractor tool, a tube for a spare bolt spring, and two flash-hider cleaning containers. A box marked with a "P" (*Petroleumskasten*) is for 1.25-liter containers of oil and petrol. Also shown is a very typical brush for cleaning weapons. In the background, the unit armorer's tool box is visible.

Box stencil marked with a "P" for *Petroleumskasten*, with the two containers for petroleum and oil for cleaning and lubricating the weapons. Two containers for spare bolt springs, *above*: for the MG 34; *below*: for the MG 42.

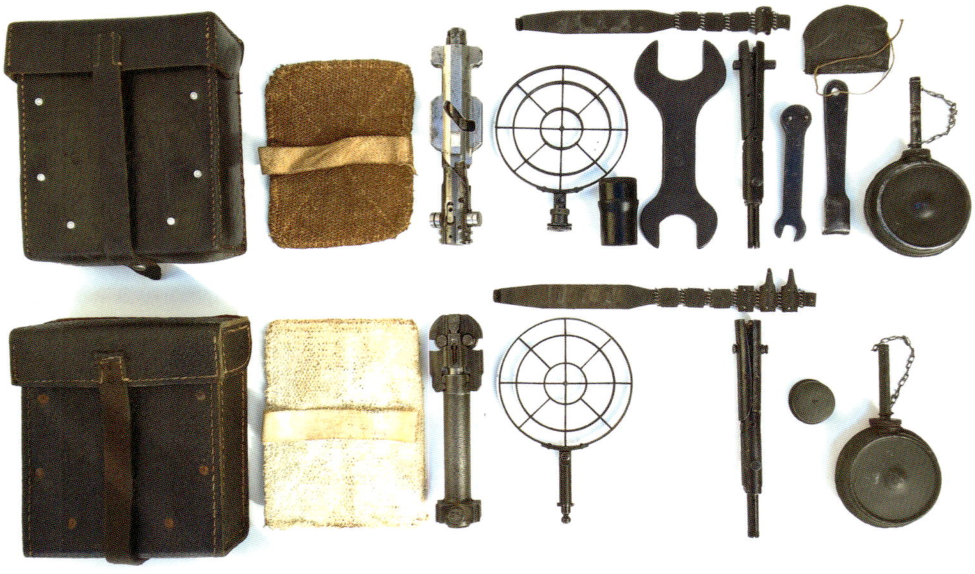

Inventory of two pouches. *Top*: early-war (1940) MG 34; *below*: end-of-war (1945) MG 42.

A range of different gunners' tool kits. *Bottom*: two early-war leather pouches. *Top*: pouches in the substitution material *Presstoff*.

- a 13 mm hook wrench (*Zapfenschlüssel* or *Zweilochmutter*) for unscrewing some bolts on the Lafette 34 model

- a starter end, which could also be used to extract the hot barrel from its sleeve

- A rubber cap (*Mündungskappe*), to prevent foreign bodies from entering the barrel. This accessory became an official part of the kit starting in 1941, when the troops of the Reich took action in Russia and North Africa. In order to economize on rubber, sachets of waterproof paper replaced the cap, which came with a tie to attach the sachet around the flash hider. These sachets (*Staubschützbeutel*) officially became part of the kit in a gunner's pouch in 1943.

- a double key, of the same type used on the MG 13, used to unblock the hexagonal bolt on the flash-hider

- a screwdriver with an angled blade (90°) (*Winkelschraubenzieher*), used both as a screwdriver for the buttstock screw and as a shell extractor

- an oil buret

Other accessories made in the units were often added to these regulation ones: for example, a chamber brush (*Patronenlagerreiniger*). This T-shaped brush was made of a single metal rod onto which the regimental armorers welded a cross-handle.

Apart from these permanent accessories, mentioned above, some were removed or added throughout the war in response to specific needs caused by the intervention in new theaters (Africa, Russia), but also simply to economize on raw materials.

The first pouch specific to the MG 34 was adopted in 1940, and in addition to the basic accessories it had the following elements:

- a caliber gauge for the 7.94 mm caliber barrel (*Kaliberzylinder*), positioned in a case held under the cover of the pouch by two spring clips

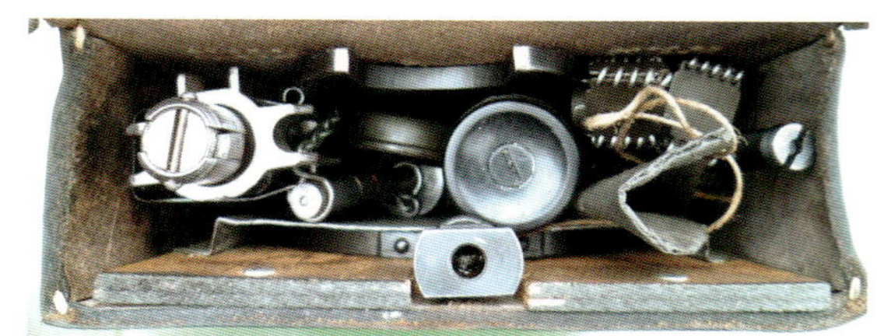

The contents of a pouch. Note that, though crowded, everything has its place. Collectors take care to complete these kits according to the date of manufacture, since the contents changed throughout the war.

Small series of *Patronenkasten*. *From the left*, a model in steel with the number of the MG, and two models in aluminum, destined for medics with the first aid kit. *Middle*: a *Patronenkasten* with the badge of the Kampfgruppe Peiper (the badge of the 1st SS Panzer Division was a shield with a key that was the personal badge of the division commander, General Sepp Dietrich (Dietrich means "skeleton key" in English).
The box second from the right is a Patronenkasten 41, in steel with a sealing joint. *Right*: An end-of-war make without electric spot-welded rivets.

Straps for ammunition boxes (Tragegurt 34). *Left*: A prewar version with large hooks pivoting on 360°. *Middle*: Two versions with different shades of canvas. *Right*: A very rare version with four straps for attaching two box-carrying bags.

- A flowers-of-sulfur applicator; the powder, mixed with the oil of the weapon, was supposed to improve the lubrication of the weapon (similar to black lead powder still used in locksmithing). The development of more-effective oils led to the removal of this applicator, which was officially decommissioned in 1944. In the theaters of operation where there were very low temperatures (Norway, Russia, etc.), the Wehrmacht phased out any lubrication of weapons parts to avoid blocking the mechanism due to the oils becoming harder.

In 1941, the composition of the *Werkzeugtasche* was modified: the flowers-of-sulfur containers and the caliber gauge stopped being included in the kit, whereas a rubber barrel cap (*Mündungskappe*), rendered indispensable by the operations in Russia and North Africa, was added.

In 1943, in order to economize on strategic materials, the rubber cap was replaced by a sachet containing twenty-five muzzle covers in waterproofed paper.

In 1944, the round oil can was replaced by a more rudimentary, rectangular-shaped one.

Several examples of spare barrel cases. *Top*: A *Laufbehälter* barrel container for two MG 34 barrels. This box is marked with the number of the MG. Next, a gray *Laufschützer* barrel protector for an MG 34 or 42 barrel. *Below*: Two sand-colored *Laufschützer* for MG 42 barrels. They are all equipped with their original carrying handles, which is quite unusual.

Range of ammunition boxes and containers. *From top left*, a belt box Gurtkasten 34 for a belt of 100 cartridges. This box was designed for armored reconnaissance vehicles. Next, a box of cartridges for armored vehicles Patronenkasten Pz34 for 250 rounds and destined for heavy mounts in bunkers or ball mounts. Also, a drum carrier Gurttrommelträger 34 with its two drums (*Trommel*) of fifty rounds each, and a Patronenkasten 36 for 150 cartridges, for the double-mount Zwillingsockel 36. *Foreground*: Two drums of fifty rounds.

Two versions of the Gurtsack, for holding ammunition on the panzer

Filling a *Trommel* with a fifty-round belt. The starter end hooks into the bracket welded under the exterior flank of the *Trommel*. *Left*: A unit marking with the number of the MG.

Protective cover for the MG 34 receiver called Bezug. This accessory also exists for the MG 42.

The manufacture of the *Werkzeugtasche* itself also evolved throughout the course of the war. The first models, entirely in blackened leather, gave way to models in natural and then synthetic leather. This synthetic version was a mixture of powdered leather, glue, and paper paste concentrated under pressure, giving rise to its name, Presstoff. It had a grainy, shiny appearance, since it was impregnated with a waterproofing varnish. This material fulfilled its role well but was not very resistant to twisting and pulling. The belt loops, shoulder straps, D-ring attachment, and strap to close the pouch were often made of real leather or, for the closing strap, in a canvas textile.

The markings made on the Presstoff were initially done with a stamping machine and tended to wear away after a short time. The markings made at the end of the war were therefore painted with a stencil, which also meant that no time was wasted engraving the stamps.

For cleaning the weapon, the gunners used the RG 34 cleaning kit for K.98k carbines.

SMALL-WEAPONS KIT

***Kleiner Waffenwerkzeugatz* (or *Waffenmeisterkasten*)**

This unit was assigned to company armorers, so they could carry out the first reconditioning immediately behind the lines. Like many other accessories of the MG 34, this group was wisely conceived to offer the maximum of possibilities with the minimum of volume. It was packed in an ammunition box (Patronenkasten 34), which facilitated its transport and handling.

This box was assigned to the NCO responsible for weapons at company level (*Waffen- und Geräte-Unteroffizier*).

Apart from the MG 34, this box meant that basic repairs and maintenance on the majority of German infantry weapons could be carried out. Some of the tools that it contained were nonetheless specific to the MG 34 and its Lafette.

A certain number of supports specific to military bicycles of the Wehrmacht (*Truppenfahrrad*) were developed to transport the MG 34 with its accessories (tripod, ammunition boxes).

Transport sling, made of a double leather strap, with a padded area at its midpoint to improve grip and comfort. A first version had a rectangular hook smaller than that of the second version, which was general purpose for the MG 34 and 42. There were three versions of hooks on the side of the jacket (the hook on the left for the Lafette carrying strap).

The box had an internal rack that when deployed exposed the main tools, held in place by clips, in positions identified with white paint.

Two drawers placed at the base of the rack meant that small tools could be stored (pin remover, screwdriver blades, etc.). A caliber gauge is placed in a case fixed by a clip under the inner side of the rack base.

Complex repairs, outside the skills of the weapons company NCO, were entrusted to the next echelon, the *Waffenmeister*: a qualified armorer of the rank of adjutant or chief warrant officer who worked with several subordinates in a workshop set up at regimental level (or, less commonly, at battalion level).

At this level, the armorers were equipped with boxes of spare parts and conserved a stock of weapons considered too damaged to be repaired. These weapons were a source of spare parts for repairable weapons. This common practice, called "cannibalization" in the French army, explains why perfectly authentic weapons have diverse original parts, which were renumbered only when there was enough time.

The mission of these regimental workshops was to restore the weapons and their mounts on site, as well as to make the modifications stipulated on a regular basis by means of technical notices sent to the units by the Waffenamt, so the weapons could be put back into service immediately and thus avoid straining logistical resources by reducing the return of weapons for repairs.

The regimental echelons did not limit themselves to procuring parts by cannibalization, but they also had boxes of spare parts (*Ergänzungskasten*) of the same size as the boxes of cartridges and identified by the letters "E," "V," or "Z," stenciled on the cover. These markings were assigned to different boxes of spare parts according to the contents. In addition, they were also equipped with large wooden boxes (*Vorratkasten*) containing multiple spare parts for the main infantry weapons in service.

Two machines for loading belts. *Top*: a Gurtfüller 34 with handle. *Bottom*: a pressure-controlled Gurtfüller 41, which loads two cartridges in the belt simultaneously. The Gurtfüller was designed for storing standard ammunition in boxes.

The signal is given, and the unit leaves the trench. The man standing in the foreground is heavily laden with a *Laufbehälter* (container for two spare barrels) for MG 34s, and at least one ammunitions box, among many other things.

CHAPTER 14

CONCLUSION

The MG 34 was a remarkably well-thought-out weapon and was designed according to a clearly defined tactical use. It was put into service with a large number of accessories that were extremely well made; in particular, the Lafette 34 mount and its sight: the MG.Z 34.

At the end of the war, many countries, including Czechoslovakia, Yugoslavia, Israel, and Norway, rushed to put into service captured German MGs for their own benefit. Other victors in the Second World War researched and tested captured German machine guns very carefully in order to design their new equipment. The MG 34, therefore, and especially its younger relation, the MG 42, along with their mounts, held a determining influence on postwar military equipment.

While it is easy to be full of admiration for the technical ingenuity of the MG 34 and the quality of its production, a more tempered approach coupled with a study of comments made by German Second World War combatants leads to the recognition of several flaws: its mechanical perfection made it costly to make and dependent on a particularly careful and rigorous maintenance regime.

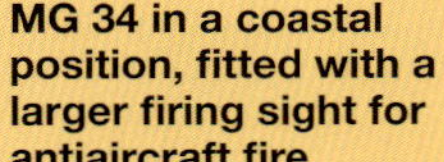

MG 34 in a coastal position, fitted with a larger firing sight for antiaircraft fire

Designers made improvements to make it a multipurpose machine gun, but that meant the weapon had to be used by well-trained personnel so that the mount and sight were used to maximum effect. Initially this did not present a problem for the Wehrmacht, victorious for the first years of the war, but started to be a disadvantage during the second half of the war, when training time had to be reduced so recruits could be sent to the front.

These factors certainly precipitated the adoption and the accelerated putting into service of the MG 42.

The MG 42 was a simpler weapon and easier to use, and it was also better suited to the conditions at the end of the war. Its high rate of fire was effective against the Soviet attack waves, but its high consumption of ammunition posed the real problem of resupplying the front lines when the transport capacities of the Wehrmacht were collapsing.

With this special edition dedicated to the MG 34 and 42, the authors are well aware that the subject has not been exhausted—first, because it is so immense, and second, because it has not always been possible to find the rare weapons and accessories that we would have liked to present.

• • •

This edition would have been impossible without the help of several French collectors specializing in German machine guns and their accessories. They wish to remain anonymous; nonetheless, we wish to express our sincere gratitude.

A special mention should also be made to the Norwegian author Folke Myrvang, who has put his vast knowledge about the MG 34 and 42 at the disposal of collectors in his two-volume *MG 34–MG 42: German Universal Machineguns*, published by Collector Grade Publications.

CLASSIC GUNS OF THE WORLD SERIES